MULTINATIONAL INDUSTRIAL RELATIONS SERIES

No. 10. European Studies
(No. 10a—Spain)

THE POLITICAL, ECONOMIC, AND LABOR CLIMATE IN SPAIN

by

MARIO GOBBO
Research Assistant
Industrial Research Unit

INDUSTRIAL RESEARCH UNIT
The Wharton School, Vance Hall/CS
University of Pennsylvania
Philadelphia, Pennsylvania 19104
U.S.A.

Copyright © 1981 by the Trustees of the University of Pennsylvania
MANUFACTURED IN THE UNITED STATES OF AMERICA
Library of Congress Catalog Number 81-52617
ISBN: 0-89546-034-3
ISSN: 0149-0818

Foreword

In 1972, the Wharton School's Industrial Research Unit established its Multinational Industrial Relations Research Program to supply:

1. key factual information and research concerning the activities, programs, policies, and potential impact of the international unions—including the "trade secretariats," communist and Christian groups, and the regional European, African, and Asian union blocs;

2. similar information regarding the International Labor Organization, the Organization for Economic Cooperation and Development, the United Nations, the European Community's Economic and Social Committee, and other transnational governmental bodies, which frequently are used for and/or support international union objectives and which have adopted codes of conduct for multinational corporations that could significantly affect international labor relations;

3. evaluation of the political, economic, and labor climate affecting investment return in countries throughout the world;

4. analysis and comparison of employee relations and public policy issues among different countries;

5. special in-depth studies, either as part of the research effort concerned with the above or separately underwritten by special information requests.

The publication of this book, *The Political, Economic, and Labor Climate in Spain*, by Mario Gobbo, marks the first such study of a European country. Four studies have been completed for Latin American countries—Brazil, Mexico, Peru, and Venezuela. In addition, studies have been done for the Philippines and the countries of the Arabian Peninsula. Studies of India, Colombia, the Central American Republics, Portugal, and Nigeria are soon to be published or underway.

Foreword

The author of this study, Mario Gobbo, was born in Colombo, Sri Lanka. He is an Italian citizen and graduated from Harvard College with a degree in organic chemistry, and also received his Master of Science degree at the University of Colorado in Boulder. After working for a period in this field, he enrolled in the Wharton School, where he received a Master of Business Administration degree and will receive his Ph.D. in industrial relations in May 1982.

The manuscript was edited by Ms. Cheryl DellaPenna, Chief Editor of the Industrial Research Unit; Ms. Mary T. Kiely prepared the index; Mrs. Margaret E. Doyle, Office Manager, handled the various administrative matters involved; and Ms. Lois A. Rappaport, then Senior Research Specialist, Multinational Studies, read the manuscript and made many constructive suggestions. The study was financed by contributions of our Multinational Research Advisory Group Information Service subscribers. Such funds are unrestricted, although it is understood that they will be used for multinational industrial relations studies. The author is, of course, solely responsible for the study's content and for the research and views expressed, which should not be attributed to the University of Pennsylvania or to the Multinational Research Advisory Group.

> HERBERT R. NORTHRUP, *Director*
> Industrial Research Unit
> The Wharton School
> University of Pennsylvania

Philadelphia
November 1981

TABLE OF CONTENTS

	PAGE
FOREWORD	iii

CHAPTER

I. INTRODUCTION ... 1

II. POLITICS IN SPAIN ... 5

    A Historical Overview ... 5

        The Second Republic and the Civil War ... 6
        End of the Civil War to the Death of Franco ... 7
        Post-Franco Spain ... 8

    Political Parties and Autonomous Regions ... 16

        Regional and Autonomous Groups ... 17

    Foreign Relations ... 20

        EEC Membership ... 21
        NATO Membership ... 21
        Other Contacts ... 22

    The Latest Elections and the Political Future of Spain ... 22

    Concluding Comments ... 24

III. THE SPANISH ECONOMY IN PROFILE ... 27

    The Infrastructure ... 27

        Transportation and Port Facilities ... 28
        Communications ... 30
        Energy and Fuel Resources ... 30
        Mineral Resources ... 32
        Agriculture and Fishing ... 33
        Industry and Manufacturing ... 36
        The Service Sector ... 39

CHAPTER	PAGE
Economic Growth	40
Inflation and the Peseta	42
The Balance of Payments and Trade	46
Wages, Unemployment, and the Job Market	54
The Role of the State	64
Investing in Spain	69
Conclusion	72
IV. SPANISH LABOR LAW: A REVIEW	75
Past Labor Legislation	79
The Constitution	80
The Workers' Statute	81
Collective Bargaining under the Workers' Statute	84
Other Labor Legislation	87
The Courts and the Labor Ministry	88
Conclusion	90
V. ORGANIZED LABOR IN SPAIN	91
Historical Overview	92
Spanish Unions Today	96
1978 Trade Union Elections	101
The Workers' Statute	103
The Acuerdo Marco	106
Latest Trade Union Elections and Other Recent Events	108
June 1981 Tripartite Agreement	113
The Major Labor Confederations	114
The CCOO	114
The UGT	122
The USO	123
The ELA/STV	124

Table of Contents vii

CHAPTER   PAGE

     Concluding Comments 124

VI. CONCLUSION 125

LIST OF TABLES

TABLE   PAGE

CHAPTER I

1. A Summary of Spain's Demography, Politics, Economy, and Labor Force 4

CHAPTER II

1. Percentage Participation at the Polls 10
2. A Profile of Spain's Political Organization 13
3. Post-Franco Era Electoral Results: 1977-1979 23

CHAPTER III

1. Total Energy Consumption 31
2. Production of Selected Minerals 33
3. Principal Agricultural Products 35
4. Main Indicators: Past Performance and Forecasts 38
5. Balance of Payments 47
6. Foreign Assets and Liabilities 49
7. Spain's Foreign Trade, by Tariff Sections 52
8. Foreign Trade by Geographical Area 53
9. Labor Market Trends 56
10. Spanish Emigration, Europe and Overseas: 1961-1978 57
11. General Indicator of Economic Activity and Social Welfare 58
12. Structure and Evolution of National Income, Gross Domestic Product and Production Factors 59

TABLE	PAGE
13. Minimum Daily Pay	61
14. Average Wages for Spanish Workers	62
15. Estimated Hourly Compensation of Production Workers in Manufacturing: Thirteen Countries, Mid-Year 1980	63
16. International Comparisons: 1979	64
17. INI's Major Industrial Companies	65
18. Spain: Corporate Tax Rates	71

CHAPTER IV

1. Main Labor Laws, Decrees, and Orders in Spain: 1926-Present	75
2. Selected Provisions of the Constitution	81
3. Selected Provisions of the Workers' Statute	82

CHAPTER V

1. Major Labor Confederation in Spain	96
2. Regional Labor Unions	99
3. Other "Independent" Trade Unions ("sindicatos amarillos")	100
4. Results of the 1978 Trade Union Elections	102
5. Results of the 1980 Trade Union Elections and Comparison with the 1978 Elections	108
6. Regional Results of the 1980 Elections	108
7. The International Trade Unions and Secretariats in Spain	116

LIST OF FIGURES

FIGURE	PAGE

CHAPTER III

1. Transportation System in Spain	29

List of Figures

FIGURE   PAGE

2. Inflation in Spain: Percent Annual Variation of the Consumer Price Index 43
3. Price Competitiveness 44
4. Exchange Rate Developments 45
5. Trend of Unemployment 55
6. Price and Wage Developments 60
7. Spanish Public Sector Holdings 66

CHAPTER V

1. Winners of Trade Union Elections (1980) 110
2. Wage, Price, and Productivity Increases in Spain, 1973-1981 115
3. Organizational Diagram for a Major Spanish Confederation 121

ILLUSTRATION

Spain 3

CHAPTER I

Introduction

Spain has always occupied a position of great importance in the history of Europe. After the trauma of the Civil War of 1931-1936, the country experienced a time of relative calm, which allowed for a period of slow rebuilding and industrialization; however, it was also a period of political stagnation under the leadership of Generalissimo Francisco Franco y Bahamonde, Caudillo (sole ruler) of the Spanish state. With his death on November 20, 1975, and the subsequent coming to power of King Juan Carlos I, grandson of Alfonso XIII,[1] also came democracy.

The new king had the vision to realize that the Spanish people were ready for a change after long years of dictatorship, and also the foresight to choose as his prime minister such a capable man as Adolfo Suarez. In various elections, the Spanish people have proved their political maturity in the last few years and now enjoy a climate which, although far from being trouble-free, is moving the country toward the status of other more industrialized and more prosperous countries of Western Europe.

It is precisely this new Spain, this reawakening of Spanish consciousness, that is of interest here. The new democracy brought more relaxed relations with countries that had opposed the regime of Francisco Franco. As a result, Spanish trade is now booming, Spain is preparing to enter the European Economic Community (EEC), banks are lining up to open subsidiaries in Spain, and new investment ventures are beginning to modernize the country. Of course not everything has run smoothly in these few years of democracy. Several separatist groups, most notably the Basques, have committed acts of terrorism and violence; rivalries between various political parties with opposed

---

[1] Eugene K. Keefe et al., *Area Handbook for Spain* (Washington, D.C.: U.S. Government Printing Office, 1976), p. 3.

ideologies have created confusion in the political arena; the newly recognized labor unions have exacerbated contention in employee-employer relations; and the military has watched with unease the birth of a new democratic system.

In this study, the economic, political, and labor situation of modern Spain is explored. Naturally some references will be made to the past to help clarify the present-day situation, but, in general, the emphasis is on the post-Franco era, with specific reference to such factors as labor relations, labor laws, the investment climate, economic developments, and other subjects considered important within the business community.

Whenever possible, footnotes have been provided to substantiate the data presented throughout this study. Some of the information, however, is the product of conversations with international labor specialists and businessmen knowledgeable of the region, as well as correspondence with Spanish unionists and personal insight. Regrettably, not all of the latter sources can be duly acknowledged in the text. (Table I-1 provides a general informational sketch of Spain.)

Introduction

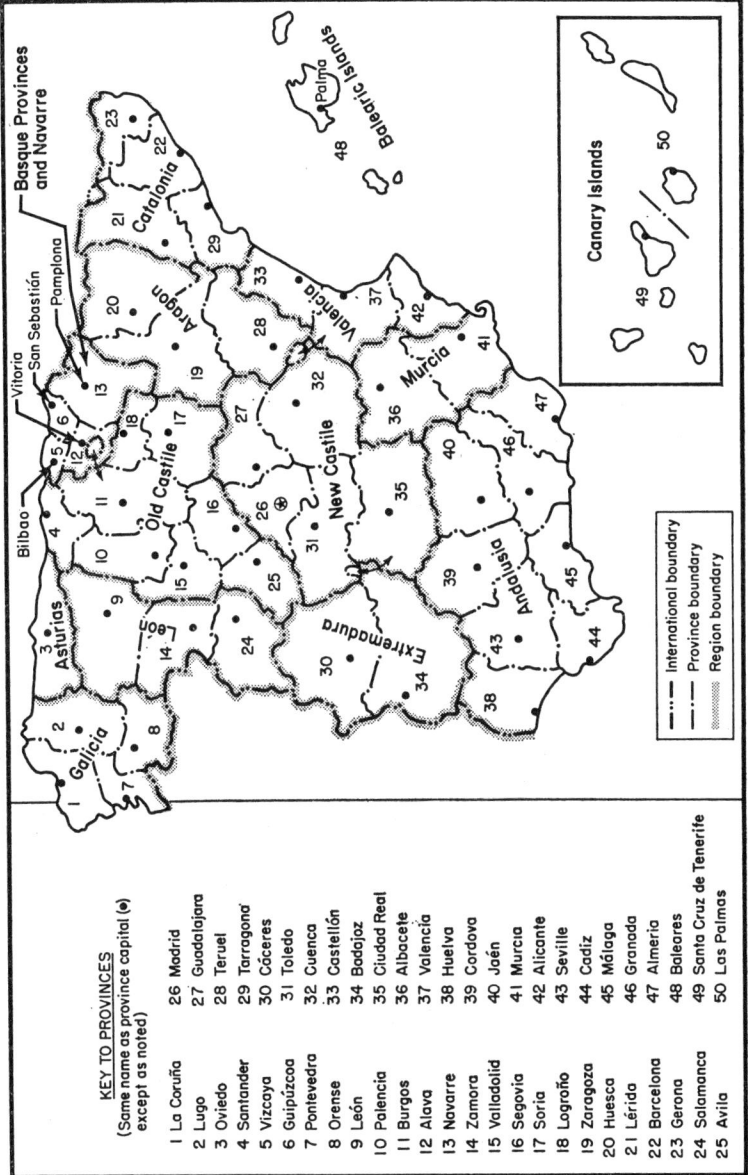

TABLE I-1
A Summary of Spain's Demography, Politics, Economy, and Labor Force

Area	194,883 square miles (504,800 square kilometers). This figure includes the Balearic and Canary Islands. It constitutes 5/6 of the Iberian Peninsula and is roughly twice the size of Oregon.
Population	37,180,000 (1979 estimate). 72 inhabitants per square kilometer. 55 percent of the population live in cities with populations of over 20,000 people.
Major Cities	Madrid (capital: 3,228,057), Barcelona (1,751,136), Valencia (707,915), Seville (589,721), Saragonza (479,845), Bilbao (431,071) (1979 estimate).
Political Regime	Parliamentary monarchy. The present king is Juan Carlos I. The Parliament (Cortes) is composed of a Lower House and of the Senate. The three main political parties are the Union of the Democratic Center (UCD), the Spanish Socialist Workers' Party (PSOE), and the Spanish Communist Party (PCE).
Economic Growth	Real GDP growth in 1980 was 1 percent. The GDP in 1979 amounted to $147.2 billion. The annual per capita income in 1979 was $3,967 (at current prices and exchange rates).
Trade	The trade balance was $4,024 billion in 1979 and widened to $12 billion in 1980. Major imports: oil products, machinery and appliances, agricultural and food products. Major exports: transport equipment, agricultural and food products, and metals and metal products.
Inflation	The annual rate of inflation, which had increased to 22 percent in 1977, eased up to 15 percent in 1980, and estimates predict that it will be around 14 percent for 1981.
Labor Force	13,482,000, of which 2.317 million are in agriculture, 4.296 million are in industry, 1.2 million are in construction, and 5.3 million are in services (fourth quarter 1979).
Unemployment	The biggest problem in Spain today, it is estimated at over 11 percent for 1980 (or 1.5 million workers).
Rate of Exchange	88.00 Pesetas=U.S. $1.00. There was an approximately 25 percent peseta devaluation in 1977; since then the peseta floated back to a pre-1977 exchange rate with the U.S. dollar, for 1979. In 1980, however, the peseta again lost 20 percent against the U.S. dollar, and is expected to weaken by a further 5-7 percent in 1981.

CHAPTER II

Politics in Spain

Spain's peculiar position as a bridge between Northern Africa and the rest of Europe and as a dividing line between the Mediterranean Sea and the Atlantic Ocean has given rise to a fascinating and colorful diversity of peoples, languages, and customs. In order to understand this diversity and its impact on contemporary Spain, the historical setting must be examined, with particular attention paid to the period following the deposition of the monarch in April 1931, a few years before the Civil War.

A HISTORICAL OVERVIEW

The marriage of Fernando and Isabel, heirs respectively of Aragon and Castile, brought about the union of two previously warring kingdoms in 1479. A few years later the Reconquista, a long struggle to free the Iberian peninsula from the rule of the Moors, who had conquered it before 800 A.D., ended. Thus Spain became a nation. This was true only in a political sense, however, because the country was (and still is) made up of a wide array of ethnic groups. These included not only Castilians, Catalonians, Galicians, and Basques, but also Arabs, who left traces of their brilliant civilization behind, as well as Jews, Aragonese, and Leonese. All were proud of their heritage, and many retained a fierce sense of independence. These different national entities within Spain tried, from time to time, to assert their independence. This separatist tendency is at the root of the autonomous movements that still exist in the Basque region and in Catalonia, as well as—if to a lesser extent—in Andalusia, Galicia, and Aragon.

The discovery of America in 1492 brought Spain to the apex of world power in the sixteenth and seventeenth centuries. Charles V and Phillip II, its two greatest monarchs, were rulers of a vast empire upon which, as was often said at the time, "the

sun never set." With the nineteenth century, however, came the
slow but inexorable decay of the Spanish empire, whose last
remnants—except for a few African possessions—crumbled during the Spanish-American War of 1898. The twentieth century
brought about a long period of instability in the Spanish kingdom, which finally ended with the establishment of a dictatorship in 1936 by Francisco Franco after a long and bloody civil
war.[1]

The Second Republic and the Civil War

Alfonso XIII, who had been king of Spain since 1886 (under
the regency of his mother Maria Christina of Austria until 1902),
abdicated in April 1931 when antimonarchist parties won a substantial vote in the municipal elections and the subsequent riots
seemed an indication of imminent civil war. The Spanish republic was proclaimed shortly thereafter, but it was not to have
a long life. The ineptitude of the last few Spanish monarchs
combined with violent strikes had created a society that tended
to become increasingly polarized into leftist and rightist factions. Subsequent elections gave power first to the Left Republicans, then to the Confederation of the Autonomous Right
(Confederación Española de Derechas Autónomas—CEDA), and
finally to the Popular Front, a coalition group composed of followers of leftist ideologies.[2]

Basically, republican Spain was divided into three factions,
all unable to fill effectively the vacuum left by the exile of Alfonso XIII. The three were the royalists, the nationalists, and
the forces of the left, which united into the Popular Front. Deep
ideological and economic differences separated the three groups.
The royalists represented the landed nobility, the nationalists
represented the young middle class, which admired the new
fascist states then emerging in Europe (Italy and Germany),
and the leftists represented the workers and the young intellectuals, followers of the Russian revolution.[3]

---

[1] Historical notes based on information contained in Hermann Kinder
and Werner Higelman, *Atlante Storico Garzanti (V edizione)* (Milano: Aldo
Garzanti Editore, 1972); and Eugene K. Keefe et al., *Area Handbook for
Spain* (Washington, D.C.: U.S. Government Printing Office, 1976).

[2] Keefe, *Area Handbook for Spain*, pp. 40-41.

[3] *Ibid.*

The followers of the left were themselves split into three groups: the pro-Moscow Communists of the Spanish Communist Party (Partido Comunista Español—PCE); the Socialists and their Workers' Party (Partido Socialista Obrero Español—PSOE), with a labor counterpart in the General Workers' Union (Unión General de Trabajadores—UGT); and the anarchists of the National Workers' Confederation (Confederación Nacional de Trabajo—CNT). Because of its anarchistic ideology, this last group was, of course, not strictly a leftist entity. It is now quasi-extinct, while the other two are still viable and powerful in Spain. The CNT grew in response both to the needs of fishing villages in Catalonia, where collective fishing was common, and to the needs of the farmers in the southeast of Spain, where communal regulation of water resources was practiced. The organization developed with utopian ideals of a worldwide collectivistic commonwealth, and lost its attractiveness only after modern capitalism brought a higher standard of living to Spain and the rest of Europe in the mid-twentieth century.[4]

It is relatively easy to understand how war finally broke out in 1936. The nationalists joined forces with the royalists, thus splitting Spain into a right and left. This division left a deep wound, the scars of which are still visible today. With forces evenly matched, the Marxists and the non-Marxists mistrusted each other, believed in the innate fallacy of the other, and unfortunately, set out to show the righteousness of their opinions by force.

The events of the Civil War need not be narrated here. Many authors, from Hemingway to a multitude of recent historians (there are many histories of the Spanish Civil War published today), have portrayed the struggles, battles, and evils of this conflict in which over 600,000 people lost their lives.

End of the Civil War to the Death of Franco

As is well documented, the war was won by the nationalists and their leader Franciso Franco. He brought peace and unity to Spain but also suppressed many freedoms. Any attempt to revive political or trade union liberties was brutally silenced. Even in this climate of outward calm, however, the Spanish people retained in their hearts old divisions and ideologies.

---

[4] Gabriel Jackson, *The Spanish Republic and the Civil War 1931-1939* (Princeton, N.J.: Princeton University Press, 1965), pp. 17-20.

Franco during his long authoritarian rule had never been able to heal the wounds of the war, and although political opposition was effectively suppressed, it was never eliminated. Political parties were outlawed. In lieu of parties Franco created the National Movement, a conglomeration of right-wing groups that he had drawn together to be his ruling faction and, with the army and the church, one of the bases of his power. Opposition groups were generally forced to operate underground, and their leaders often lived in exile.[5]

With the aging of the Caudillo, a title conferred on Franco to recall that of the old tribal chief of pre-Roman Spain, came the inevitable weakening of the National Movement, the monolithic political party of post-Civil War Spain, which was also known as the Falange. By 1973/74 there were already signs that the kettle of Spanish politics was ready to boil over. Admiral Luís Carrero Blanco, Franco's prime minister and probable successor, was assassinated in December 1973, allegedly by Basque terrorists. Much social unrest followed, including several strikes, which were then illegal. This state of affairs continued notwithstanding repression and soon began to worsen.

It is no wonder then that many received the news of Franco's death on November 20, 1975, after a long illness, with a certain sense of relief, in the hope that things would change for the better. Of course many also feared the eruption of violence and the renewal of pre-Civil War divisions. Fortunately, the passage to democracy proceeded much more smoothly than all had anticipated.

Post-Franco Spain

There was no so-called "Portugalization" of Spain, i.e., a minority of the population did not radicalize the situation after many years of dictatorship. Juan Carlos I was designated as successor to Alfonso XIII by Franco, who considered Juan Carlos's father, Don Juan (who is still alive today), too liberal to assume power. Time revealed, however, that Juan Carlos was to be a cautious, but eventually liberal, monarch himself.

The steps toward democracy were gradual. First, the king, who had assumed power just before Franco's death, astutely named in early 1976 Carlos Arias Navarro, a Franco appointee, as prime minister. This was probably done to avoid a clear break with the past, which could have caused trouble with right-wing sympathizers and the army.

---
[5] Keefe, *Area Handbook for Spain*, p. v.

Second, the Cortes (the Spanish Parliament), a unicameral rubber-stamp body under Franco, approved a measure for several political parties to organize legally [6]—the Spanish Communist Party was one of the exceptions—and called a referendum for political reform. The referendum was held in December 1976, and the proposed formation of a new Cortes, allowing for some form of proportional representation and composed of lower and upper houses,[7] was overwhelmingly approved by the electorate.

Third, the king asked Arias Navarro to resign as prime minister [8] and shortly thereafter appointed Adolfo Suarez, a younger, more modern man to take his place in July 1976. Fourth, in a bold move, the Communist Party was legalized in April 1977.

Finally, as the crowning achievement of post-Franco Spain, the first free political elections since 1936 were held on June 15, 1977, and, contrary to common expectations, there were no outbreaks of violence nor any confusion. The Spanish people voted with great composure and with an amazing sense of balance. The middle-of-the-road Union of the Democratic Center (Unión de Centro Democrático—UCD) gained a plurality, followed by the moderate, leftist Socialist Workers' Party. The more extreme Spanish Communist Party and the right-wing Popular Alliance (Alianza Popular—AP) trailed as distant third and fourth, respectively. *The Economist* summarized the election results as follows:

> Extremes tend to beget extremes. But Spain's Disraeli, Mr. Adolfo Suarez, has succeeded in harnessing what might have been an irresistible pressure for revolution after 40 years of right-wing dictatorship into support for his own moderate conservative party. In Spain's general election on Wednesday Spaniards gave a vote of thanks to their prime minister for allowing them the right to choose their government.
>
> With 75% of the votes counted, Mr. Suarez's Centre Democratic Union looked set to win some 170 seats out of 350. His main rival, the Socialist Worker party (PSOE), was far behind, heading for some 115 seats. The right-wing Popular Alliance, and the Communists were expected to get 15-20 seats each. Among the other

---

[6] Roger Matthews, "Cortes approves parties reform," *Financial Times*, June 10, 1976, p. 7.

[7] Roger Matthews, "Hazardous path to democracy," *Financial Times*, December 6, 1976, p. 29.

[8] Henry Giniger, "Spanish premier resigns, apparently at King's wish," *New York Times*, July 2, 1976, p. A-4.

200-odd parties, only the Popular Socialists, the Christian Democrats and a far left group had won as much as 1% of the vote.[9]

Since that election, the Spanish people have been able to exercise their democratic right several times. There have been elections in 1978 [10] and 1980/81 to select workers' bargaining representatives in public and private enterprises employing a minimum of six employees, a referendum for the approval of a new constitution in 1978, new parliamentary elections in March 1979, and, for the first time since the pre-Franco Spanish republic, municipal elections in April 1979. This balloting has been generally free of disruption from terrorist acts by the several extremist and separatist groups. All has proceeded with calm, and, as in other democratic countries, the Spanish people have chosen their representatives in a most predictable fashion. Attendance at the polls has fallen since the June 1977 euphoria for the new found freedom, as people settled back into their routines and gained a certain degree of political apathy, which can be seen from the increasing rate of absenteeism at the polls (see Table II-1).

TABLE II-1
Percentage Participation at the Polls

Election	Date	Percent Participation
General Elections	June 15, 1977	78.4
Constitutional Referendum	December 6, 1978	67.7
General Elections	March 1, 1979	66.4
Municipal Elections	April 3, 1979	60.0

Source: "La Alegría de la Izquierda," *Cambio 16*, No. 384 (April 15-21, 1979), p. 10.

Throughout the past few years, two men have safely steered the Spanish nation away from possible storms: King Juan Carlos I and especially Adolfo Suarez, the leader of the UCD and, until recently, prime minister. Juan Carlos wisely chose to step out of the spotlight and appoint Suarez, a man acceptable to all, very capable, but little known at the time. Suarez was

---

[9] "Spain's Centre Holds," *The Economist*, Vol. 263, No. 6981 (June 18, 1977), p. 55.

[10] Benjamin Martin, "Labor and Politics in Spain Today," *Relations Industrielles*, Vol. 34, No. 1, p. 108.

able to bring full democracy to Spain without angering the military. He was able to allow a slow return of political and trade union freedom without upsetting the left, who had hoped for a speedier solution. In addition, he managed to keep the Basques and other separatist forces from causing too much trouble without either repressive measures or too much laxity.

This was accomplished in a relatively short time, but not without a great deal of trouble. In a country where tempers flare up quickly and where old Civil War enmities may lie dormant under the surface, as evidenced by the "Galaxia" plot of the summer of 1978, by the recently attempted coup, and by the latest planned coup, economic and political woes always make front page news. The shockingly high inflation rate and increasing unemployment gave Suarez many headaches in the past, and still trouble his successor, Calvo Sotelo.

The leftist terrorists of the Antirevolutionary Group of the First of October (Grupo Revolucionario Antifascista Primero Octubre—GRAPO) and especially the Basque separatists of Euskadi Ta Alkartasuna (ETA) have committed many political murders and bombings in an attempt to cause panic, force military repression, and stimulate popular uprisings. This is the typical "politic of terror," similar to that of the Red Brigades in Italy and the Bader-Meinhoff group in Germany implemented by a few fanatics and, hopefully, destined to fail.

Spain's history is still being written today. The elections in which the UCD retained parliamentary plurality had hardly been filed when an important event took place at the last PSOE congress, held in May 1979. The PSOE membership adopted an overtly Marxist label that expressly supports the class struggle. This resolution was strongly opposed by party leader Felipe Gonzalez, who resigned in protest. In an emotional speech, Gonzalez mentioned that such an overtly Marxist stand would not only be "electoral suicide" for the PSOE, but would also raise the specter of the old Civil War split between Marxist and non-Marxist factions.[11] Fortunately, such a division never materialized, and, in a special congress held in October 1979, Gonzalez triumphantly returned to power. Shortly thereafter, having pulled the PSOE back to the center-left, he became one of the sponsors of the recently approved Workers' Statute (see

---

[11] Robert Graham, "Gonzalez snatches victory from defeat," *Financial Times*, May 22, 1979, p. 2.

Chapter IV), the first real piece of labor legislation since the Franco years.

The devolution process for Spain's regions and more major economic problems forced Suarez to reshuffle his cabinet in an attempt to placate government critics. This decision, however, backfired and opened up deep wounds within the ruling party, the UCD.[12]

As a reaction to further criticism from all sides and a deepening split within the UCD, Suarez replaced his personal friend, Fernando Abril Martorell, with Leopoldo Calvo Sotelo as economics minister, in an attempt to isolate himself from conflict.[13] This move failed to solve the situation, as did the cancellation of the second congress of the UCD (which was to have been held in Palma de Majorca) because of an air traffic controllers' strike.

Critics claimed that "the air traffic dispute [was] being used to permit Sr. Adolfo Suarez . . . to postpone the congress and defuse the anticipated criticism of his leadership." [14] A cool reception marred by strikes during Suarez's visit to the Basque region and further protest against his leadership finally prompted the prime minister to resign on January 29, 1981.

The man appointed to succeed him was Calvo Sotelo. After much debate, he was finally accepted by the UCD leadership. He is on good terms with the king and had been named minister both in Arias Navarro's and Suarez's cabinets.

It is interesting to note that, in July 1936, the assassination of Calvo Sotelo's uncle, José Calvo Sotelo, a prominent rightwing monarchist, was one of the sparks that ignited the Spanish Civil War.[15] Somewhat ironically, after newspapers described Calvo Sotelo's nomination as a victory for the right,[16] an anachronistic colonel of the Guardia Civil, Spain's paramilitary

---

[12] Robert Graham, "Minor shuffle reveals major split," *Financial Times*, May 7, 1980, p. 2.

[13] Robert Graham, "Spanish cabinet in major reshuffle," *Financial Times*, September 9, 1980, p. 18.

[14] Robert Graham, "Cancellation of spanish party congress provokes outcry," *Financial Times*, January 29, 1981, p. 4.

[15] James M. Markham, "Spanish chief born to power," *New York Times*, February 12, 1981, p. A-7.

[16] Robert Graham, "A qualified victory for the right," *Financial Times*, February 10, 1981, p. 2; and James M. Markham, "A turn to the right looms in Spain," *Wall Street Journal*, February 15, 1981, p. 2E.

police force, took over the Spanish Parliament in an attempt to restore the dictatorship of the Franco years.

The prompt intervention of King Juan Carlos, commander-in-chief of the armed forces, saved the day. The Spanish monarch "firmly rejected" the revolt [17] and ordered the army to crush any sign of rebellion. Only General Milans del Bosch managed to take control of the city of Valencia before order was restored.

Specters of civil war were raised, especially because many high military officers either were involved, such as General Armada, a friend of Juan Carlos, or hesitated about which side to take before obeying the king's orders. When calm was restored, Calvo Sotelo was voted by the Cortes to be prime minister. Many claim that he is only at this post to keep Suarez's seat warm. The truth of this statement cannot yet accurately be judged, but one thing is certain: while he occupies that seat, Calvo Sotelo will have many problems to solve of and on his own.

Trouble has already started with the resignation of all seven top police officials, who were "angered by the public outcry over the death in police custody ... of a suspected member of the militant Basque separatist organization, ETA." [18] In addition, it was recently discovered that a group of generals had planned yet another coup, this time to take place during a reception given by Juan Carlos. Fortunately, the revolt never went beyond the planning stage. As if this were not enough, unemployment has reached alarming proportions, surpassing the 11 percent mark, and shows no signs of abating. The future of any Spanish premier is clouded by many problems, and strong leadership is absolutely necessary to steer a course of economic recovery and political peace. (An overview of Spain's current political organization is provided in Table II-2.)

TABLE II-2

A Profile of Spain's Political Organization

Administration	Spain is a social and democratic state, advocating as higher values of its legal order justice, liberty, equality, and political pluralism. The political makeup of the Spanish state is that of a parliamentary monarchy.

---

[17] "Spain's cabinet and over 355 legislators are taken hostage in an attempted coup," *Wall Street Journal*, February 24, 1981, p. 3.

[18] Robert Graham, "Spanish police resignations a major challenge to Calvo Sotelo," *Financial Times*, February 18, 1981, p. 20.

TABLE II-2 (continued)

Parties	The formation and activities of political parties are free as long as the constitution and the law are respected. The internal structure of each party must be democratic. The main nonregional parties are: Union of the Democratic Center (Unión de Centro Democrático—UCD); Spanish Socialist Workers' Party (Partido Socialista Obrero Español—PSOE); Spanish Communist Party (Partido Comunista de España—PCE); Democratic Coalition (Coalición Democrática—CD); National Union (Unión Nacional—UN). The main regional parties are: National Basque Party (Partido Nacionalista Vasco—PNV); the Basque Left (Euzkadiko Ezquerra—EE); Convergence and Union (Convergencia i Unio—CiU), also called Catalonian Democratic Convergence (Convergencia Democrática Catalunia—CDC); Andalusian Socialist Party (Partido Socialista Andaluz—PSA); United People of Canaria (Unión del Pueblo Canario—UPC); Regionalist Aragonese Party (Partido Aragonez Regionalista—PAR).
Executive	The parliamentary monarchy in Spain is, in many respects, similar to the system in Great Britain. The king, Don Juan Carlos I de Borbon y Borbon, is the chief of state but has little power. He has a hereditary title and a largely honorary function. He is supposed to sanction and promulgate laws, assemble and dissolve the Cortes, decree elections, and propose the candidate to the position of prime minister, all in accordance with specific rules that leave him almost no freedom of action. The real executive power is held by the prime minister, now Leopoldo Calvo Sotelo, who can initiate policies and laws. Usually the prime minister is the leader of the political party that holds a plurality in the Congress, or lower chamber of the Cortes. Some regions have their own form of parliament. For example, there is the Generalitat in Catalonia and the Disputación Foral in Navarre. These and other regional institutions will gain importance now that the autonomy statutes are being approved.
Legislative	The Spanish Parliament, which is officially called Las Cortes Generales, or Cortes for short, is made up of two chambers: the Senate, or upper house, and the Congress, or lower house. The members of the Cortes are elected by direct universal suffrage to four-year terms. The members of the Congress (disputados) are elected as follows: a minimum of one for each province, and the rest in proportion to the population in each province. Four senators (senatores) are elected for each province,

TABLE II-2 (continued)

	with special provisions for autonomous communities, Ceuta and Melilla (remnants of the Spanish Moroccan possessions), and the Canary Islands.
Judicial	The Spanish Supreme Court is seated in Madrid and is called the Tribunal Supremo. It encompasses six courts: the Court of Cassation, for civil and commercial actions, the Criminal Appeals Court, three Courts for Contentions of Administrative Matters, and the Court of Appeals in Social Matters. In addition, there are Territorial High Courts and local courts. Labor disputes can be appealed to the Court of Appeals in Social Matters. Labor courts are organized as follows: Magistratura de Trabajo (labor court). There exists at least one of these in each of the fifty Spanish provinces. Tribunal Central de Trabajo (Central Labor Court). Formed by labor judges with at least ten years' experience in the labor courts, it is divided into four chambers: one for dismissal cases, one for labor cases excluding dismissals, and two for social security cases. It deals with cases of appeal from the labor courts. Sala de lo Social del Tribunal Supremo (Social Chamber of the Supreme Court). It is composed of eleven judges and is the highest level of labor courts. There is no appeal proper from the Central Labor Court to the Supreme Court, but the general attorney of the kingdom is empowered to present a very unique kind of appeal, "recurso en interés de la ley" (appeal in the interest of the law), if he believes that the legal rules established in the Central Labor Courts are erroneous.
World Organizations	Spain belongs to the United Nations, the Organization for Economic Cooperation and Development, the World Bank, the International Monetary Fund, the International Energy Agency, the World Tourism Organization, the International Telecommunications Satellite Consortium, and others.

Sources: *Background Notes: Spain* (Washington, D.C.: U.S. Department of State, December 1977); "All the Spains: a Survey," *The Economist* (insert), November 3, 1979; R. Blanpain, ed., *International Encyclopaedia for Labour Law and Industrial Relations*, Vol. 4 (The Netherlands: Kluwer, 1977); "A Survey of Spain," *Financial Times*, December 20, 1979; *The International Yearbook & Statesmen's Who's Who, 1981* (East Grinstead, England: Kelly's Directories Ltd., 1981), p. 423.

POLITICAL PARTIES AND AUTONOMOUS REGIONS

The multiplicity of political parties has its roots both in pre-Civil War divisions and in present-day aspirations for regional autonomy. The birth of the UCD, however, is a special case. Its formation was the outcome of a desire to join the moderate, center-right forces into a homogeneous body as a new version of the pre-Civil War coalition, the United Popular Front. Much has changed since then, however, and the party leaders, Santiago Carillo for the Communists (PCE), and Felipe Gonzalez for the Socialists (PSOE), have made their own imprint on their respective parties. The PCE has tried to erode the strength of the PSOE, and the moderate stand of Carillo contributed in great part to the March 1979 electoral gains of the Communists. Gonzalez also attempted to be moderate and thus gain strength for his party by eroding the left wing of the UCD, but his attempt was far less successful, and the PSOE failed to make any gains at the polls.

The electoral failure brought about a redefinition of the PSOE to a more Marxist stand, and consequently led to the resignation of the leader who advocated a more centrist line, as already mentioned. As a result, the PSOE found it more and more difficult to appear distinct from the PCE, and this effected two new developments. First, it fostered more cooperation between the PSOE and the PCE at the local level (municipalities). Second, the socialist trade union, the UGT, began to fear that it was "losing ground to the Communist controlled Confederation of Workers Commissions (CCOO). The increasing organisational strength and political weight of CCOO at the expense of UGT is also weakening an important part of what should be the PSOE's natural constituency—especially if it sees itself as a class party." [19]

These developments were reversed, however, at the latest trade union polls when the PSOE, once again led by Felipe Gonzalez and adopting a more moderate stand on all issues, seemed to gain in popularity, while the UGT completely recovered from earlier losses and managed to pull neck and neck with the CCOO. Apparently, the drift toward a realistic conservatism has brought the Socialists, both the PSOE and the UGT, to the forefront once again. More than ever, they may now be enjoying a period of ascendancy.

---

[19] Robert Graham, "The rank and file demands a say," *Financial Times*, May 17, 1979, p. 3.

Until recently, the right had been represented by the Popular Alliance, now split into the Democratic Coalition (Coalición Democrática—CD) and the National Union (Unión Nacional— UN) of Franco, both led by nostalgic Blas-Piñar. The CD has given outside support to the governments of both Suarez and Calvo Sotelo and thus finds itself in the mainstream of the governing group. The Socialists (PSOE) and the Communists (PCE) form the opposition group, but any real cooperation at the national level between the two is not expected, as both will battle for the position of the real "alternative on the left."

A development worthy of mention rocked the PCE at the beginning of 1981 and may threaten it with a sharp break in its ranks. During the fifth congress of the United Socialist Party of Catalonia (Partido Socialista Unificado de Cataluña—PSUC), a federated member of the PCE, PSUC delegates voted to avoid any references to Eurocommunism. This means that the PSUC is essentially differing from the line taken by PCE chief Santiago Carillo. The vote reflects a partial victory for the pro-Soviet faction of the PSUC. It should be noted that the PSUC provides about 25 percent of all PCE membership. The pro-Soviet faction, however, was unable to elect its own candidates for the posts of president and secretary general of the party, but it will certainly manage to cause serious problems for Santiago Carillo in the upcoming tenth PCE congress.[20]

In the interest of being thorough, small splinter parties, which elicit more curiosity than anything else and carry little, if any, weight, should be mentioned. Included are the Communist Revolutionary League (Lega Comunista Revolucionaria—LCR), the radical Spanish Socialist Party (Partido Socialista Español— PSE), the Party of Spanish Workers (Partido de Trabajadores Español—PTE), who joined with the Revolutionary Organization of the Workers (Organo Revolucionario de los Trabajadores— ORT) to win some support in the April 1979 municipal elections,[21] and others.

Regional and Autonomous Groups

Last but not least, as they carry a great deal of weight in Spanish politics, are the regional and autonomous parties. They

---

[20] "El V Congreso del PSUC," *El País*, January 7, 1981, p. 8; and Robert Graham, "Catalan challenge to Carillo's leadership," *Financial Times*, January 7, 1981, p. 2.

[21] *Cambio 16*, April 1-7, 1979, p. 3.

form—especially since the March 1979 elections—a rather large group and are a force which must be taken into consideration both by the left and center. Each one of these parties has widely different interests, and therefore, they are unlikely to form a cohesive group. By supporting various causes, however, some may be able to swing the balance to the left or right. An example of this occurred when the Andalusian Socialist Party (Partido Socialista Andaluz—PSA) allowed Suarez to have a clear majority in Parliament before his resignation by supporting the UCD government.

The Basque and the Catalonian nationalist parties are significant. Fostering the widely diverse interests of their two respective regions, they are both a thorn in the side of any central authority. In Euskadi (as the Basques call their homeland), the situation is further complicated by Navarre, one of the four Basque provinces that has held, since the Civil War, a special status for siding with Franco's Nationalists. The other three provinces, Vizcaya, Alava, and Guipuzcoa, sided with the Republicans and are the provinces where most of the trouble caused by the ETA is taking place. Because of the differences existing between Navarre and the rest of Euskadi, the government decided that the issue of Navarre being designated an autonomous Basque province—where the left and the Nationalists would have a clear majority—would be decided by a referendum. This solution seems unacceptable to the more extremist Basques, who probably support the ETA and the leftist Euzkadiko Ezquerra (EE) and who would like to see the formation of a separate Marxist Basque state. This situation is indeed unfortunate, and it is exasperated by events such as the leader of the party Popular Unity (Herri Batasuna—HB), Telesforo Monzon, being elected to the Cortes while in prison for "apologia for terrorism." [22] The largest Basque nationalist party is the Partido Nacionalista Vasco (PNV), a moderate group led by Carlos Garailkoetxa, one of the key men who engineered the historic agreement on Basque autonomy and who is now Lendakari, or president of the provisional Basque government.

The Catalonian problem is far less complicated, especially because there seem to be no terrorist groups in that region. Although Union and Convergence (Convergencia i Unio—CiU), the local regional party, led by Jordi Pujol, is pushing for enhanced

---

[22] Alberto Ronchey, "La Vittoria de Suarez," *Corriere della Sera*, March 3, 1979, p. 1.

powers for the Generalitat,[23] the situation is a political one and does not threaten to give way to violence. The moderate stand of the CiU is well exemplified by the fact that, often the CiU has supported the government and has limited its opposition to the issue of devolution.[24]

The Andalusian Socialist Party (PSA) is led by Rojas Marcos, a man who, above all, advocates Andalusian autonomy. With the slogan "Andaluz, if you don't vote for your own land, who will?," he managed to raise the PSA from a nonexistent representation to five seats in the Cortes. In addition, the mayor of Seville, Andalusia's capital, is a member of the PSA. Pushing for an autonomy statute similar to that for the Basque provinces and Catalonia (see below), Marcos does his best to promote Andalusia. These attempts include making close contacts with the Islamic world, which has been linked with the region since the Moorish conquest, in the hopes of attracting petrol dollars.[25]

A little-mentioned problem of regional autonomy is the aspirations in that direction of the Canary Islands, an archipelago off the western coast of Africa. The United People of Canaria (Unión del Pueblo Canario—UPC) is pushing for autonomy, and most likely some of its supporters would view even total independence favorably. The UPC has little weight outside its home territory, although it did manage to muster enough support to get one seat in the Cortes during the March 1979 elections.

The Aragonese Regionalist Party (Partido Aragonez Regionalista—PAR) and the Galician National Group (Bloque Nacional Popular Galego—BNPG), from the Aragonese and Galician regions, respectively, represent special regional interests in the Cortes.

To cope with these centrifugal forces, and hard-pressed to find a solution to the terrorism of ETA-Militar (the most violent faction of the ETA), Suarez placed each of Spain's thirteen component regions on an equal footing for the determination

---

[23] The Generalitat is the historical governing body of Catalonia, so called after a medieval parliament of the Kingdom of Aragon Catalonia. It was reestablished for the first time since the pre-Civil War Spanish republic at the end of 1977.

[24] Jackson, *The Spanish Republic*, pp. 77 and 165.

[25] David Gardner, "Rojas Marcos," *Financial Times Survey: Spain*, December 20, 1979, p. IX.

of home rule. This was a way of selling autonomy to the Basques, since they would be the first to obtain a regional government statute. The idea was presented as a long overdue decentralization plan for the whole of Spain.

In accordance with this plan, the government proposed devolution statutes for the Basque provinces (excluding Navarre) and for Catalonia. These were approved by referendum in October 1979. After that, however, the government backstepped on its proposals and offered to grant less autonomy to other regions applying for their own statutes. This would have created a second division of autonomies, which can cause many problems. Through strikes and general unrest, the Communists and Socialists protested the autonomy statute offered to Galicia. Similarly, 500,000 Andalusians marched in December 1979 to demand a statute at least as generous as the Basque and Catalonian ones.[26]

The Galician autonomy statute was approved in November 1979 despite strong misgivings about its vagueness as compared to the statutes of the Basque and Catalonian regions.[27] An agreement on Andalusian autonomy was reached in October 1980 by the political parties, but an outright solution to the problem is still not in sight.[28]

The importance of Spain's regional disputes can hardly be underestimated, given its past history, the present problem of terrorism, and the political implications of granting too much autonomy to independence-minded regionalists. The central government must tread a thin line in order to appease everyone, and this is proving to be a very difficult task.

FOREIGN RELATIONS

Economic and political relations between Spain and the rest of the world are entering a phase of rapid expansion after the isolationist years of Franco. Spain has applied for membership in the European Economic Community (EEC), has intensified trade with South America, is considering entering the North Atlantic Treaty Organization (NATO), and has begun to make the first contacts with communist countries.

---

[26] *Ibid.*, "Devolution is State's major challenge," p. VIII.

[27] Robert Graham, "Galicia autonomy statute approved," *Financial Times*, November 11, 1979, p. 2.

[28] Robert Graham, "Agreement reached on Andalusian autonomy," *Financial Times*, October 24, 1980, p. 2.

EEC Membership

From an economic point of view, membership in the EEC would bring both advantages and disadvantages, but it would definitely bolster the new constitution and symbolize Europe's approval of Spain's new order.[29] This is the opinion, at least, of all the political parties, from the right-wing Democratic Coalition to the Communists. Negotiations were begun in the early months of 1979, and it is only a question of time before Spain will officially join the European Community. Spain's highly protected industry and its vigorous, low-cost agricultural production will present problems, however. It will need to lower tariffs, and an agreement will have to be reached on agricultural products. This will not be easy and already several disagreements between Spain and the EEC have arisen, some over Spanish dumping of steel products, others over citrus fruit exports. ("Dumping" occurs when products are sold at a loss in foreign markets.) In general, however, all these are relatively minor problems, since both democracy and a satisfactory level of economic development are present today in Spain, and these are the crucial factors involved in EEC membership.

NATO Membership

NATO membership, on the other hand, presents a more difficult problem. "Joining NATO would break Spain's tradition of avoiding military alliances which could commit it to the defence of other countries."[30] In addition, the PSOE is opposed to the move, and, if a left-wing group were to gain power, it would take Spain out of NATO. Gibraltar poses a problem of its own, with Britain supporting its independence and Spain insisting on sovereignty over it. Militarily Spain stands little to gain from membership, since NATO's protective umbrella is unofficially provided because of the country's geographical position.[31] Therefore, negotiations will proceed slowly, as diplomats both in Spain and in NATO sit back and let the debate take its course. Further developments can be expected only when the Spain-United States defense agreement is reviewd in 1981.

---

[29] "Spain at Europe's Door," *The Economist*, Vol. 268, No. 7044 (September 2, 1978), p. 48.

[30] "Will They Join NATO?," *The Economist*, Vol. 268, No. 7044 (September 2, 1978), p. 51.

[31] *Ibid.*

Other Contacts

Spain is also interested in becoming an associate active member of the South American Andean Group and in increasing trade with Mexico, for its petroleum. This interest has been highlighted by the recent visits of Suarez to Venezuela [32] and of King Juan Carlos to Latin America.

Other foreign policy goals include improving ties with less developed countries and with the Arab world. In addition, Spain supports negotiating a settlement in the Saharan conflict between the Algerian-backed Polizario and Morocco in an attempt to find a peaceful solution to the problem of Ceuta and Melilla, the two Spanish enclaves on the North African coast. Special care has also been taken to improve contacts with radical states, evidenced by Spain's participation in the nonaligned conference in Havana, Cuba, as well as its contact with radical organizations, in an effort to ensure that they do not abet Spanish terrorist organizations.

Also worthy of mention is Spain's new treaty with the Vatican to replace the Concordat of 1953, in accordance with the new Spanish constitution, and, for the first time since the Civil War, a visit to the Soviet Union by the Spanish foreign minister. Aside from its political implications, the visit will most likely help Spain increase trade with the Soviet Union, which is now at a very low level.[33] As other examples of Spain's new international relations: the king accepted an invitation to visit China, and the Palestine Liberation Organization (PLO) leader, Yasir Arafat, visited Spain in September 1979.

It will indeed be interesting to observe the continuing ramifications of this "opening up" of Spain, a country which, only ten years ago was firmly refusing any contact with the outside world and insisted on living in the past.

THE LATEST ELECTIONS AND THE POLITICAL FUTURE OF SPAIN

The March 1979 election that brought about the present division of forces in Parliament is admirably summed up by Paolo

---

[32] "Spain develops economic links with Latin America," *Latin America Economic Report*, Vol. VI, No. 38 (September 29, 1978), p. 300.

[33] David Slatter, "Spanish minister visits Moscow," *Financial Times*, January 18, 1979, p. 2.

TABLE II-3
Post-Franco Era Electoral Results: 1977-1979

Political Party	Number of Seats 1977 Congress	Number of Seats 1979 Congress	Number of Seats 1979 Senate	Popular Vote for Congress % in 1977	Popular Vote for Congress % in 1979
UCD	165	168	120	34.71	35.2
PSOE	118	121	65	29.24	29.4
PCE	20	23	—	9.24	10.8
CD	16	9	2	8.39	5.5
UN	—	1	—	0.30	—
CDC, CiU	11	9	1	—	—
PNV	8	7	8	1.69	1.5
HB	—	3	1	—	9.9
EE	1	1	—	—	—
PAR	—	1	—	—	—
PSA	—	5	—	—	1.7
PSUC	—	—	2	—	—
PSC	—	—	5	—	—
UPC	—	1	—	—	—
Others	5	2	4	n.a.	—
PSP [a]	6	—	—	n.a.	—

Sources: Alberto Ronchey, "La Vittoria di Suarez," *Corriere della Sera*, March 3, 1979, p. 1; "Le glissement à droite de M. Suarez illustre l'évolution de l'électorat," *Le Monde* (section hebdomadaire), February 22-28, 1979, p. 5; "A Latin Adenauer for Spain," *The Economist*, Vol. 269, No. 7052 (October 28, 1978), p. 53; "We Are the Very Model of a Modern Moderate Electorate," *The Economist*, Vol. 270, No. 7071 (March 10, 1979), p. 57; "Spanish voters endorse moderate Suarez policy," *Financial Times*, March 3, 1979, p. 2.

[a] Joined with the PSOE after 1977 election.

n.a. = not available.

Bugialli, a journalist for the *Italian Corriere della Sera* (see Table II-3 for complete electoral results).

One victor: Adolfo Suarez, with his UCD. Notwithstanding the dark forecasts of the astrologers of politics, he increased by two the number of seats for his party with respect to the past elections. More importantly he increased the advantage he held over the socialists, his closest competitors: from 41 to 49. One defeated: Felipe Gonzalez. Calculating his party as fused with that of Tierno Galvan [Popular Socialist Party (Partido Socialista Popular—PSP)], he lost four percentage points. The communists of

Santiago Carillo increased their seats by two. A clamorous debacle: that of the old AP of Fraga Iribarne. Presenting itself to the electors with a new name: the Democratic Coalition, it lost almost half of its votes and fell from 16 to 9 seats. [34]

It has been observed that the major problem of the new government will be that of the autonomous parties. Indeed, that will be true, as there has been no real left versus center-right standoff. There was never any doubt that the Spanish people, when presented with either the "alternative on the left," a moderately socialist but nonetheless socialist society, or with Western European society, would choose the latter. This is somewhat similar to what happened recently in Italy. In both countries the left is strong, but the majority of people prefer the present system to a socialist experiment, which gives no guarantee of success. There is also no doubt, however, that the Spanish people who live in regions with a history of independence, or at least of autonomy, want their relative freedom from Madrid, and Madrid will need to find a solution.

A solution must also be found to stop the bloodshed caused by the ETA, to stop the infighting in Parliament, and to allow the central government to devote all of its energies to decreasing unemployment and inflation and provide a stable environment so that the whole country can prosper. This will be especially necessary if Spain plans to enter the EEC in the near future and thus bring its economy and standard of living up to par, perhaps not with Germany, but at least with Italy and Ireland.

CONCLUDING COMMENTS

In summary, Spain is a nation that has proved it is capable of voting as well as other countries with much longer democratic traditions and of developing into an industrialized, "Western style," economic nation. There still remain several problems, however, which present no easy solution. First and foremost is the question of autonomy. Second, many members of the military are still unsatisfied with democracy; another attempted coup is not totally out of the question. Third is the very high rate of unemployment, which, if not decreased in the near future, can cause great discontentment in the country as a whole. Finally,

---

[34] Author's translation from Paolo Bugialli, "Cosí il Voto," *Corriere della Sera*, March 3, 1979, p. 5.

the country is plagued by an ever higher inflation rate, which erodes any desire to invest and thus to expand the economy. (The economic problems will be treated in more detail in the next chapter.)

In the political sphere, Calvo Sotelo has a compact majority in Parliament, which is composed of his own party, the UCD, and the right-wing CD, and which may be supported by the autonomous PSA, the PNV, and the Catalonian CiU. This coalition will give the government a chance to accomplish something despite both the PSOE and the PCE being firmly entrenched in the opposition and ready to use all the weapons at their disposal, including trade union pressure from the UGT and the communist Comisiones Obreras (CCOO).

The latest political events may at first bewilder an outside observer, but there is logic in the apparently chaotic and confused sequence of events. The Spanish government, backed by center-right parties, tried at first to weaken the PSOE by making a de facto alliance with the PCE in many parliamentary debates. The PCE was, of course, happy to oblige the government in the hopes of eroding the PSOE's left flank. Then, the government found its proposal for a Workers' Statute supported by the PSOE and opposed by the PCE. This resulted from the fight for trade union supremacy between the socialist UGT and the communist CCOO. At this point, the government found it more profitable to back the UGT with its more moderate stand and to weaken the CCOO, which up to now, has been and still is the largest and most intransigent of all the trade unions. (More will be said about this political maneuvering in Chapter V.)

The attempted coups and the trouble with the military all stem from a general dislike of democracy shown by many high officers of the armed forces. A major conflict can most likely be avoided, however, because of the large consensus that the new Spanish order has drawn from leftist and rightist groups alike, as well as the firm prodemocratic stand of Juan Carlos. Yet the king must be careful from now on, since he has directly involved himself in the political woes of the country and can no longer be seen simply as a symbol outside the political arena. In other words, Juan Carlos has compromised his position of neutrality as leader of "all the Spains" and should attempt once again to remove himself from the inevitable sectoral disputes.

The days of the Moncola Pact, an agreement between all the major parties and (though not explicitly) the unions to allow a virtual freeze on all wages so that a smooth transfer to a fully democratic society could proceed without obstacle, are gone. Although modified by the difficult economic situation, labor strife and political infighting is to be expected on all fronts. The situation, in other words, is now normal.

To conclude, one must note that, as in other Western nations, Spain has had the good fortune to have the right man in charge at the right time: "There has been some admirably deft helmsmanship lately by captains Giscard d' Estaing of France, Helmut Schmidt of Germany, Constantine Karamanlis of Greece, and Adolfo Suarez of Spain."[35] It is believed that such good steering will continue from Calvo Sotelo, Suarez's successor. It is also maintained that Suarez will continue to figure prominently in Spanish politics, however indirectly. This is fortunate for Spain because Suarez is a modern, intelligent man who has been blessed with both wisdom and good fortune and who has been described, perhaps not unfittingly, as Spain's Adenauer.[36]

---

[35] "A Remarkable Steadiness," *The Economist*, Vol. 270, No. 7071 (March 10, 1979), p. 14.

[36] "A Latin Adenauer for Spain," *The Economist*, Vol. 269, No. 7052 (October 28, 1978), p. 53.

CHAPTER III

The Spanish Economy in Profile

The worldwide recession and subsequent slow recovery are the main factors that have caused impaired growth, falling investment, and an alarming rise in unemployment during the last few years in Spain. In addition, Spain's rate of inflation has been one of the highest in the industrialized Western world, resisting all attempts by the government to curb it. Domestic policies did not entirely "come to grips with increasing disequilibria in the economy during a period when priority was accorded to fundamental institutional and political reforms."[1] With the 1979 elections confirming the center-right Union of the Democratic Center (Unión de Centro Democrático—UCD) in power, a coherent economic program should be feasible, even though the recently attempted military coups and the subsequent right-wing drift of the new prime minister might destabilize the situation somewhat. Increasing militancy from the trade unions, the recent oil-price hikes, and the generally depressed state of the world economy, however, make it very difficult for Spain to solve its problems in the near future.

From an economic point of view, Spain should be watched closely. With a gross domestic product (GDP) of $197 billion, which places it eleventh in the world,[2] and a population of almost 37 million, it provides "a significant market of unmatched growth."[3]

THE INFRASTRUCTURE

Spain is becoming more and more like an industrialized European country and "steadily less like those charming travel-book

---

[1] Organisation for Economic Co-operation and Development, *OECD Economic Surveys: Spain* (Paris: OECD Publications, June 1978), p. 5.

[2] *Ibid.*, "Basic Statistics: International Comparisons," April 1981.

[3] "Spanish exports," *Financial Times*, July 4, 1979 (advertisement), p. 13.

watercolours."[4] This is mostly because of the above-average growth of the gross national product (GNP), which averaged 7.3 percent a year in real terms between 1961 and 1963.[5] In this section, the present state of transportation and port facilities, communications, mineral resources, industry, agriculture, etc. will be examined in detail before discussing current economic data.

Transportation and Port Facilities

Spain's railroad system comprises a total of approximately 17,300 kilometers (10,000 miles). About 13,500 kilometers are run by the state-owned National Network of Spanish Railroads (Red Nacional de los Ferrocarriles Españoles—RENFE).[6] Curiously, the RENFE network has rails that are wider than the standard European gauge. As in the Soviet Union, this was done in Spain to slow down possible troop and supply movements in case of a foreign invasion. In addition to RENFE, there is a standard gauge railroad system run partly by the Ministry of Public Works and partly by twenty-two private companies.

The structure of the Spanish railroad network is similar to that of a wheel with spokes radiating from the center. Madrid, the hub of the system, is connected by radial lines with La Coruña, Bilbao, Barcelona, Valencia, Seville, and the Portuguese border. This radial structure, complete with transverse links, ensures a maximum of connections with a minimum of lines, which reduces the costs of using the system.[7]

If compared with the modern autobahn system in Germany or the Italian autostrade, the highway network is not yet up to par, even though much progress has been made in recent years. There are 83,000 miles of roads and highways. Of these, 50,000 are under national control and 33,000 are maintained by the provinces.[8] Approximately 25 kilometers of road exist for every 100 square kilometers of surface, compared with an European aver-

---

[4] "The New Spain: A Survey," *The Economist*, Vol. 263, No. 6970 (April 2, 1977), p. 42.

[5] Alison Wright, *The Spanish Economy 1959-1976* (Plymouth, U.K.: The Macmillan Press Ltd., 1977), p. 1.

[6] Ramon Tamames, *Introducción a la Economía Española* (Madrid: Alianza Editorial, 1973), p. 319.

[7] *Ibid.*, p. 322.

[8] Eugene K. Keefe et al., *Area Handbook for Spain* (Washington, D.C.: U.S. Government Printing Office, 1976), p. 68.

The Spanish Economy in Profile

age of 55 kilometers. Also, there are only 4 kilometers of road for every 1,000 inhabitants, compared with 9 for the rest of Europe.[9] Like the railroad system, this network has a radial structure. Both the projected and most recently built "autopistas de peaje" (turnpikes) are, however, mostly concentrated in the north, the industrial Basque region, and on the eastern coast—the center of Spanish beach resorts. Other major highways include links from Madrid to Valencia, from La Coruña to Pontevedra, and from Cadíz to Cordoba.[10] (Figure III-1 maps the transportation system throughout Spain.)

FIGURE III-1
Transportation System in Spain

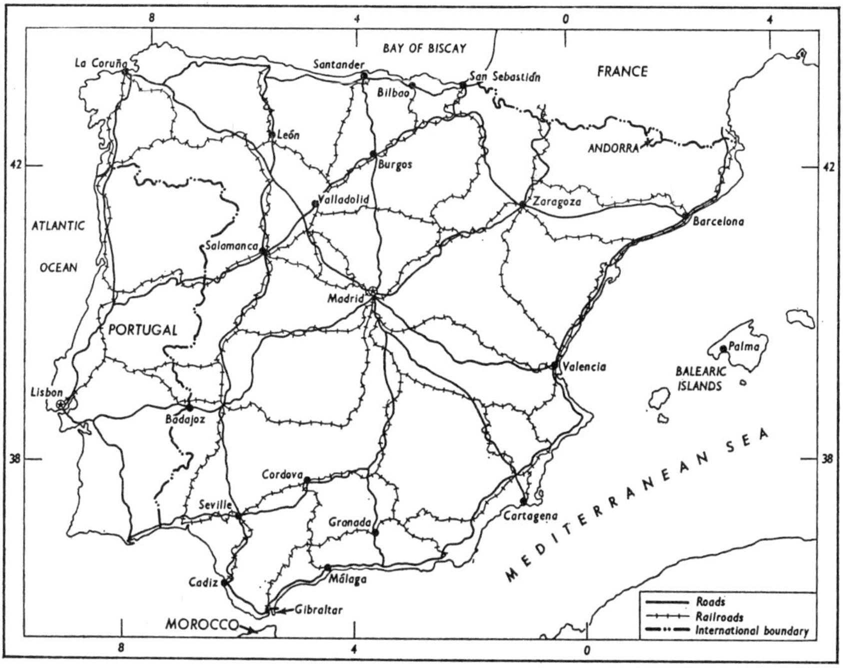

Source: Eugene K. Keefe et al., *Area Handbook for Spain* (Washington, D.C.: U.S. Government Printing Office, 1976), p. 69.

Civil aviation has become well developed in the last few years. The main airports are situated in Madrid and Barcelona, and from there flights are scheduled to most major world cities.

[9] Tamames, *Introducción a la Economía*, p. 325.
[10] *Ibid.*, p. 331.

Iberia, the national airline, has just undergone a process of modernization and today flies to eighty-two airports in forty-two countries, concentrating on Spain's local area and on the American continent.[11]

Spain also possesses a large merchant marine fleet, which, in 1974, was ranked fourteenth in the world. The tanker fleet is ranked eleventh, and the shipbuilding industry is fifth after Japan, Sweden, the United States, and the United Kingdom.[12] Barcelona, Bilbao, Valencia, and Algeciras are the busiest ports on the mainland. Important harbors include Las Palmas in the Canary Islands, Palma de Mallorca in the Balearic Islands, and Ceuta on the northern coast of Africa across from Gibraltar.[13]

Communications

The radio and television systems are controlled by the state in Spain. Some criticism has been levelled in the past toward ex-Premier Suarez and the UCD for using this control of the media to their advantage in political campaigns, and for trying to play down the increase in terrorism by Basque terrorists. In contrast to the severe censorship practices of the Franco days, however, movies, magazines, and newspapers have been liberalized. On the whole, there is a high degree of sophistication in the Spanish communications network, similar to that of other Western industrialized countries, with satellite links to the rest of the globe and news agencies from many foreign nations, including the Russian TASS and two from the United States.[14] In 1977, there were 239 telephones and 184 television sets per 1,000 inhabitants, compared with 293 and 268, respectively, in France and 718 and 571 in the United States.[15]

Energy and Fuel Resources

"Consumption of energy has increased rapidly since 1960 as a concomitant of Spain's rapid industrial growth. Spain is deficient

---

[11] "Special Section: Spain," *Business Week*, No. 2479 (April 18, 1977) (advertisement), p. 25.

[12] "Shipbuilding countries act to aid the industry in time of trouble," *Wall Street Journal*, March 8, 1979, p. 1.

[13] Keefe et al., *Area Handbook for Spain*, pp. 70-71.

[14] *Ibid.*, pp. 160-61.

[15] "Basic Statistics: International Comparisons," *OECD Economic Surveys: Spain*, April 1980.

in energy resources because of its lack of sufficient oil reserves, dwindling supplies of easily accessible coal, and inadequate water power."[16] In addition, there are only three nuclear plants in Spain, and, although four more are planned,[17] opposition to these may hinder or at least delay their construction. After the Three Mile Island incident in the United States, there have been violent protests, including several bombings—especially in the troubled Basque region—against construction of new nuclear plants.[18]

Spain has been one of the slowest countries to realize the consequences of the 1973 oil price increase and to do something about the subsequent energy shortage, which has recently been exacerbated by further increases in the cost of petroleum and by public outrage against nuclear power. "Between 1963 and 1973 energy demand increased 8.6 per cent a year, and since then it has continued to increase by 4 per cent per year. Spanish energy consumption, per unit of production is now among the highest of any OECD country."[19] (Table III-1 lists energy consumption by type of fuel for selected years.)

TABLE III-1
Total Energy Consumption
(in thousands of metric tons or coal equivalents)

Item	1977	1978	Percent of Total 1962	Percent of Total 1978
Coal	15,173	15,333	42.1	15.17
Petroleum	65,248	67,527	33.2	66.82
Nuclear Power	2,013	2,419	—[a]	2.40
Natural Gas	1,713	1,759	—[a]	1.74
Hydroelectricity	13,966	14,017	24.7	13.87
Total	98,113	101,055	100.00	100.00

Sources: *Situación*, August-September 1979 (monthly publication released by the Banco de Bilbao), p. 41; Eric N. Baklanoff, *The Economic Transformation of Spain and Portugal* (New York: Praeger Publishers, 1978), p. 84.
[a] Negligible amount.

[16] Keefe et al., *Area Handbook for Spain*, p. 333.

[17] "España 1985: Doce Centrales Nucleares," *Cambio 16*, April 15, 1979, p. 45.

[18] Jane Monahan, "Spain split on Basque atom reactor," *Wall Street Journal*, April 8, 1981, p. 33.

[19] Jimmy Burns, "Slow reaction to energy crisis," *Financial Times*, December 13, 1978, p. 10.

The long-awaited passage of the National Energy Plan (NEP) by the Cortes in the summer of 1979 brought a sigh of relief to many. In the wake of the recent Organization of Petroleum Exporting Countries (OPEC) oil price increases, the NEP went through with an unexpectedly high majority backing. The NEP provides for the completion of seven nuclear plants to add to the three already existing, so that, by 1987, Spain will have a minimum nuclear capacity of 10,500 megawatts.[20] The government will also try to encourage the development of new, autonomous sources of energy in addition to nuclear power. Strategic coal reserves will be created, and energy planners foresee a continued increase in coal consumption after the foreseen 26 percent consumption hike in 1980.[21] Natural gas, solar energy, hydroelectric power, and even biomass and geothermal resources are being investigated and, where possible, expanded.[22] Massive investment in this sector is planned in an attempt to reduce the 70 percent dependence of Spain on imported fossil fuels and to reduce to under 50 percent the national contribution of oil to the energy supply. The task is obviously an arduous one; however successful, Spain, like other Western nations, will have to cope with energy becoming more expensive and less available. Economic expansion will consequently slow down; only vigorous government action will prevent unemployment from reaching disastrous proportions.

Mineral Resources

The mineral wealth of the Iberian peninsula was what originally attracted Carthagenians and Romans, as well as earlier settlers, to colonize Spain. In recent years, however, the importance of the mining sector has been steadily decreasing. "The number of workers in the mining industry showed an absolute decline from 153,000 in 1963 to 133,000 in 1971. In 1969 mining contributed only about 1 percent of GDP compared to about 10 percent in 1930," [23] and it has declined since then.

---

[20] David Gardner, "Nuclear energy policy forges ahead," *Financial Times*, December 20, 1979, p. VI.

[21] *Ibid.*

[22] *Ibid.*

[23] Keefe et al., *Area Handbook for Spain*, p. 336.

The main minerals extracted in Spain today are: mercury, of which Spain is one of the world's foremost producers; sulfur obtained from pyrites, which are also mined for copper, iron, lead, and zinc; and coal, the production of which declined from 15 million metric tons in the late 1960s to only 10 million metric tons in 1974.[24] Other minerals found in smaller quantities are: manganese, uranium, phosphates, salt, tin, and wolfranite.[25] Table III-2 gives a brief outline of the major mineral products extracted in Spain.

TABLE III-2
Production of Selected Minerals
(in metric tons)

Mineral	1972	1977
Coal		
Anthracite	3,013,010	3,760,522
Mineral	8,050,650	8,114,575
Lignite	3,068,409	5,812,868
Antimony	138	331
Bauxite	3,089	4,754
Zinc	89,433	98,316
Copper	36,117	35,962
Tin	379	642
Iron	3,351,184	4,122,109
Mercury	1,633	926
Lead	69,443	65,540
Uranium (U_3O_8)	150	254
Tungsten (WO_3)	457	388

Source: Ministerio de Economía, *España 1979: Anuario Estadístico* (Madrid: Instituto Nacional de Estadística, 1979).

Agriculture and Fishing

Spain experienced a record wheat harvest in 1978. The subsequent increased agricultural production (8 percent with respect to 1977) helped save the Spanish economy that year. This beneficial outcome, however, cannot hide the enormous problems that burden Spanish agriculture. In 1979, Spain registered a decrease in agricultural production in real terms of about 3.2 percent,

---

[24] *Ibid.*

[25] Tamames, *Introducción a la Economía*, pp. 240-41.

while in 1980, a record 6.7 percent increase in output was recorded. A bad drought at the start of the year threatens agricultural output for 1981, thus illustrating the dangerous fluctuations that plague this sector.[26] In many regions the land is badly or not sufficiently exploited. There has been an enormous emigration, especially of young farmworkers, from the land to the cities. This industry has historically been very much neglected. Civilian employment in the agricultural sector was 20.2 percent of total employment in 1978,[27] or approximately 2.6 million workers. By contrast, in 1962 there were 4.5 million farmworkers, contributing 39.1 percent of the labor force.[28] These problems are compounded by the natural acidity of the land, the lack of large rivers for irrigation, and the mountainous nature of the Spanish terrain.

Notwithstanding all these difficulties, the revenue from production in this sector ran at about $4.5 billion in 1978, which made Spain the world's largest exporter of farm produce.[29] Despite this supremacy, however, Spain paid for only about 75 percent of its agricultural imports with exports in 1978,[30] and the balance of payments on the agrarian sector closed with a deficit of more than 91,000 million pesetas (66 P=U.S. $1).[31] The government has so far been incapable of rectifying the situation.

> The Ministry [of agriculture] has lately been accused of overstaffing, with mediocre people more concerned with power than performance, of lacking independence and stature within the administration as a whole, and of planning without acting. Indeed, it is inescapable that many Spanish farm reforms lack teeth.... Until something positive occurs to improve their efficiency and their livelihoods, the farmers will continue to regard announcements, such as that of last November [1978], about farming reforms as representing no more than pieces of paper moving around the comfortable corridors of Madrid.[32]

---

[26] *Situación*, January 1980 (monthly publication released by the Banco de Bilbao), p. 2; *ibid.*, February 1981, p. 1.

[27] "Basic Studies: International Comparisons," *OECD Economic Surveys: Spain*, April 1980.

[28] Keefe et al., *Area Handbook for Spain*, p. 310.

[29] "The farmers and their grumbles," *Financial Times*, December 13, 1978, p. VIII.

[30] *Situación*, January 1979, p. 12.

[31] *Ibid.*, February 1979, p. 17.

[32] "The farmers and their grumbles," p. VIII.

The Spanish Economy in Profile

Table III-3 provides a list of major Spanish agricultural products. Competitive sectors such as wine, citrus fruits, and olive oil exist alongside others whose yields are very low, such as grain, where the nineteen quintals per hectare fare very badly against the forty-two quintals per hectare average in the European Economic Community (EEC).[33] This is due to the fact that very labor-intensive methods are still employed in Spanish agriculture, and in general, it enjoys protective measures that shelter it from foreign competition.

TABLE III-3
Principal Agricultural Products
(in thousands of metric tons)

Product	1975	1978
Wheat	4,302	4,837
Barley	6,728	7,995
Rice	379	384[a]
Corn	1,794	1,909
Legumes	492	524[a]
Potatoes	5,338	5,247[a]
Sugar Beets	6,337	8,478
Cotton	140	99
Sunflower Seeds	416	473
Tobacco	26	26[a]
Alfalfa	13,286	13,867
Tomatoes	2,488	2,348[a]
Onions	821	979
Oranges	1,991	1,612
Apples	1,012	1,000
Pears	413	445
Almonds	255	299
Peaches	284	450
Bananas	361	359
Wine[b]	32,465	28,271
Olive Oil	455	416
Milk	5,504	5,607[a]
Meat	1,889	2,205[a]

Source: *Situación*, January 1979 (monthly publication released by the Banco de Bilbao), p. 10.
[a] Banco de Bilbao estimate.
[b] In thousands of hectoliters.

[33] John Cherrington, "Spanish farming: untapped potential for raising output," *Financial Times*, May 25, 1979, p. 25.

It is precisely these measures and the opposition of Italian and French farmers to competition from Spanish agricultural products that provide one of the major stumbling blocks to Spain's entry into the EEC. On the other hand, Spanish producers complain of unduly higher taxes imposed by the EEC on agricultural products from Spain. A case in hand is the tax on citrus fruits. "While Spain pays 12 per cent tax on citrus entering the EEC, its two chief competitors, Israel and Morocco, get away with 5 and 4 per cent respectively."[34] In the long run, however, Spain stands to gain from EEC membership, and some sort of compromise will most certainly be worked out for the agricultural export-import problem.

Fishing is of considerable importance in Spain, especially along the northern coast of the Iberian peninsula. "As far as gross tonnage is concerned, the Spanish [fishing] fleet is the third largest in the world and the first in Western Europe, and alone represents three thirds of the Nine's [EEC countries] fleet."[35]

Industry and Manufacturing

The main industries now operating in Spain are those of car manufacturing, steel, textiles, chemicals, shipbuilding, electrical appliances, leather goods, and construction. On the surface, the industrial situation seems similar to that of European countries such as France and Italy, but closer accounting reveals a generally decaying industrial panorama.

> The real reflection of the recession that is ending its fourth year in Spain is in the sorry state of much of the industry. The number of bankruptcies has multiplied alarmingly, while the plight of major sectors such as steel and shipbuilding, badly hit by the worldwide fall in demand, has often worsened.[36]

Thus was the situation for 1978. There was a small recovery at the end of the year, but it failed to gather momentum. The increase in labor costs, the rise in oil prices, the appreciation of the peseta and the subsequent loss of export competitiveness all were factors that, although predicted,[37] were difficult to combat

---

[34] "Spanish citrus: bitterness at EEC import levies," *Financial Times*, May 10, 1979, p. 39.

[35] *Europe*, No. 2592, January 8/9, 1979, p. 6.

[36] David Gardner, "Industry in a long recession," *Financial Times*, December 13, 1978, p. IX.

[37] *Informe Economico 1978* (annual publication released by the Banco de Bilbao), p. 110.

and inevitably brought both greater inflation and unemployment, thus slowing down industrial growth for 1979 and 1980.

Industrial production was up by only 2 percent in 1978, 2.3 percent in 1979,[38] and only 1 percent in 1980. This should be compared with an annual 7 percent increase for the previous five years.[39] Gross capital formation dropped by 3 percent in 1978, grew by only 0.2 percent in 1979, and accelerated to a 1.5 percent growth in 1980.[40] The GDP grew by only 3.2 percent in 1978,[41] while it further decelerated to a 1.6 percent growth rate for 1979 and a 1 percent rise for 1980.[42] All these figures point to a widening industrial gap between Spain and the rest of Europe. For purposes of comparison, it should be noted that Spanish steel and electricity consumption were about one-half that of France in 1977 and that France registered a 4 percent increase in its industrial production and a 3.5 percent increase in gross capital formation in 1979.[43]

Lest we paint too abysmal a picture of Spanish industry, it must be pointed out that the latest forecasts (summarized in Table III-4) predict a situation for 1981 no worse than that in other Western industrialized countries. This cautious optimism is substantiated both by the new National Energy Program (1978-1987), under which electric power production will increase from 100 billion kwh (kilowatt/hour) to 150 billion kwh, and by the new investments planned by foreign companies, such as General Motors (GM). In June 1980 GM signed a contract to build an automobile plant and a components factory, for a total investment of $1.6 billion; 10,000 direct and 25,000 indirect jobs will be created by this project.[44]

Signs of malaise still remain, however. Unemployment is continually on the increase, inflation has not been substantially

---

[38] *Economic Report 1979* (annual publication released by the Banco de Bilbao), p. 15.

[39] "Spain," *Business Europe*, March 9, 1979, p. 79; *ibid.*, January 19, 1979, p. 21.

[40] *Ibid.*, February 6, 1981, p. 47.

[41] *Ibid.*, September 7, 1979, p. 286.

[42] *Situación*, January 8, 1980, p. 2; "Spain," *Business Europe*, February 6, 1981, p. 47.

[43] "Spain," *Business Europe*, June 8, 1979, p. 182.

[44] *ABC* (Edición Semanal Aerea) (Madrid), June 21, 1979, p. 24.

TABLE III-4
Main Indicators: Past Performance and Forecasts

	Percent Change over Preceding Year		
	1979	1980	1981[a]
Gross Domestic Product	1.8	1.0	1.5-2.0
Industrial Production	2.3	1.0	2.0
Private Consumption	1.9	1.0	1.5-2.0
Gross Fixed Capital Formation	0.5	1.5	3.0
Public Consumption	5.5	6.5[b]	n.a.
Inflation Rate	17.0	17.0	14.0-16.0
Wages	20.0	16.0-17.0	13.0-16.0
Unemployment	9.0	11.7	n.a.

Sources: "Spain," *Business Europe*, Vol. XXI (February 6, 1981), p. 47; *ibid.*, Vol. XX (August 8, 1980), p. 253; *ibid.*, Vol. XX (February 15, 1980), p. 55; Robert Graham, "Rise in Spanish unemployment to over 11%," *Financial Times*, August 7, 1980, p. 2.
n.a. = not available.
[a] Forecasted changes.
[b] Approximation.

abated, and the pace of foreign investments seems to have slackened in the last few years. For example, Fiat's plans to take over Spain's largest car producer, Sociedad Española de Automoviles de Turismo (SEAT), which employs 32,000 people, and to transform it into a more efficient and export-oriented concern,[45] were cancelled.

In the public sector, the National Institute of Industry (Instituto Nacional de Industria—INI) is planning to reshuffle its shareholdings in sectors such as vehicle production and data processing and is increasing its stake in steel, coal, and heavy industries (shipbuilding in particular)[46] (i.e., it is planning to help out industries close to bankruptcy and avoiding sectors where foreign investments will improve the situation). More will be said about the INI and other state-owned industries in the section "The Role of the State," in this chapter.

One of the main problems confronting Spanish industry today is the technological dependence of Spain on other, more industrialized nations, such as the United States, Japan, and West

[45] Robert Graham, "Poised for dynamic expansion," *Financial Times*, June 14, 1979, p. 21.

[46] "Spain," *Business Europe*, August 25, 1979, p. 265.

Germany.[47] In order to effect the rapid industrialization process in the 1960s and 1970s, Spain had to acquire most of the necessary technology, which brought about an increasing deficit in the payments for technology transfers. The main reason for this need of technology transfers is that the many small- and medium-sized industries that constitute a large portion of Spain's industry are unable to set up their own research and development programs. In addition, the government and large firms have so far been unable to coordinate their activities and provide the necessary information for the development of a viable technological program.[48] Notwithstanding all these problems, Spanish employers have so far demonstrated innovativeness and a surprising vitality, and it seems certain that they will be able to pull industry out of the doldrums in the future.

The Service Sector

It will come as little surprise that tourism ranks first in the Spanish service sector. Almost 40 million people visited Spain in 1978, and this figure set a record that surpassed by 5 million the previous high mark, set in 1973.

In 1979 the number of people entering Spain dropped by about 2.5 percent, perhaps principally due to the Basque separatists' bombing campaign, high inflation, and labor disputes in the tourist industry. But the receipts kept rising, and it is estimated that $68 million was netted in that year.[49] The great influx of currency resulting from these hordes of vacationers constitutes a substantial positive item in the balance of payments. The tourist authorities are beginning to realize, however, that the industry cannot expand much more unless there is improvement of the facilities and a restructuring of the whole system. Many people must be drawn away from the overcrowded beaches to the interior, more stringent regulations must be adopted, and the water supply must be brought up to par with tourists' needs. In addition, if inflation is not slowed down and the appreciation of the peseta is not halted, Spain's reputation for being inexpensive will be tarnished, which will turn away many tourists in the years to come.

---

[47] *Situación*, April 1979, p. 9.

[48] *Ibid.*, p. 11.

[49] Robert Graham, "**Fewer** tourists generate bigger income," *Financial Times*, December 20, 1979, **p.** XII.

Two interesting developments have taken place in the banking sector, which occupies second place in the Spanish service industry. First, the Bank of Spain, in conjunction with 108 other banks, instituted a "Bank Hospital" designed to take over ailing banks to restore them to financial health. It is called the Banking Corporation (Corporación Bancaría), and it capitalized 500 million pesetas, which it split fifty/fifty between the banks involved and the Bank of Spain. It is not very well liked by any group, but no alternative acceptable to both the bankers and the politicians could be found.

The second development concerns the radical increase (quadrupling) of foreign banks operating in Spain. This followed the government's decision in June 1978 to allow foreign banks other than those already established to set up in Spain. The result should be a 10 percent increase in the number of banks, and many fear that this will increase the tensions in the interbank market, even though substantial restrictions have been placed on the activities of the foreign banks.[50] On the whole, the banking sector showed a general decline in profitability despite the banks' margin on operating costs averaging 5.1 percent, rather high for international standards.[51]

The transport sector has registered a substantial increase in air traffic in the past few years, while the number of passengers and amount of freight transported by trains has tended to level off.[52]

ECONOMIC GROWTH

Following the trend set by other Western economies, Spain experienced yet another year of recession in 1980. As in Italy or West Germany, the 2.7 percent real GDP growth for 1978 did not give rise, in 1979, to a mild recovery, and 1980 showed only a 1 percent increase over the previous year. Because of the continued slackness of the industrial sector, the latest OPEC oil price increases, the fluctuating agricultural growth, and the disruptive effects of the political uncertainties that led first to the resignation of Adolfo Suarez and then to an aborted coup, the GDP is not expected to gain by more than 1.5 percent in 1981.

---

[50] "World banking—Spain: New overseas links," *Financial Times*, May 21, 1979, p. XIII.

[51] Robert Graham, "Banks expect a tough future," *Financial Times*, December 20, 1979, p. II.

[52] *Economic Report 1978*, p. 39.

The government under Suarez made an attempt to revive the economy by proposing an economic plan that contains some short-term measures mixed with medium-term policies, designed to liberalize Spain's economy in view of its entry into the European Common Market. This economic program, known as Programa Económico del Gobierno (PEG), reaffirmed the need to use tight money policy as a means of economic control and to expand credit while reducing the interest rates. In addition, the government plans to control public sector spending, indeed an arduous task, especially because of a rising social security budget and because of the special fund that provides payments to depressed areas such as Andalusia.[53] The present government, headed by Calvo Sotelo, will try to follow these general lines in its economic policy. The economy still shows no signs of an upturn, however, and implementation of the above measures will be difficult.

The labor sector presents problems typical of countries with a split trade union movement that has close political ties to parties expressing a leftist ideology. The Moncloa Pact, which was signed for 1978, was an agreement between all political parties to hold wage increases below 22 percent. This pact was not entirely successful, but it eventually led to a decrease in inflation for 1979 and to the subsequent settlement of most wage contracts at an average increase of 13-14 percent in 1979. The 1980 wage agreements were regulated by the new Workers' Statute, by the pact concluded between the General Workers' Union (Unión General de Trabajadores—UGT) and the Employers' Confederation (Confederación Española de Organizaciones Empresariales—CEOE), and by the June 1981 Social Contract between the government, the CEOE, and both the UGT and the Workers' Commissions (Comisiones Obreras—CCOO). (These developments and other labor-related issues will be treated more extensively in the following chapters.)

Interestingly, as of early 1981, the Spanish unions seem to be approaching collective bargaining with a much more conservative stance. Spanish workers apparently endorsed the UGT-CEOE agreement by voting for the UGT in greater numbers than ever before during the latest trade union elections. The communist CCOO, which until June 1981 had shunned any agreement with the government or the CEOE, reversed its stand by signing the

---

[53] Robert Graham, "Economy faces a bleak year as activity stagnates," *Financial Times*, December 20, 1978, p. II.

Social Contract. The heavy CCOO losses and concomitant UGT gains undoubtedly forced the CCOO to adopt a more moderate line and follow the Socialists in signing some sort of labor agreement. This decrease in union militancy and the decisiveness with which the government of Calvo Sotelo seems ready to tackle the economic woes will hopefully bring about a slow improvement in Spain for 1981.

The projected GDP growth varies between 1.5 and 2.5 percent. This is not enough, however, to absorb the projected 1.5 million unemployed at the end of 1981. The government plans to accelerate the energy plan and to implement a housing program in order to stimulate employment. The public sector is very small in Spain, constituting about 10 percent of the GDP, and so the government is really powerless to stimulate the economy unless the private sector "begins to show a willingness to reinvest. So far there is no sign of this." [54]

Inflation and the Peseta

The liberalization of Spain after the death of Franco, which allowed for trade unions and for a more open economy; the money supply explosion in the early seventies; and the tremendous increases in the prices of oil and other prime materials were the main factors that led to an accelerated inflation during the seventies. The recent downtrend seen in the consumer price index (CPI) for 1979 and 1980 is probably due both to the decrease of inflationary pressure from wages registered in 1978-79 and to tight money policy, and it can be expected that the trend will continue in 1981 unless the public sector deficit continues to grow and the price of oil resumes its steep climb. (Figure III-2 shows graphically the trend of the CPI in Spain in recent years.) The wholesale price index increased around 10-11 percent in 1979, which also constitutes a drop from the 14 percent hike registered in 1979.[55]

Price controls have always been one of the favorite weapons against inflation in Spain. Ex-Premier Adolfo Suarez at first wanted to maintain price controls only on basic goods and services, given that the price controls were rather ineffective. Opposition from consumer groups and labor forced him to weaken his

---

[54] Robert Graham, "Better decision-making by cautious new team," *Financial Times*, December 2, 1980, p. III.

[55] *Informe Económico 1979*, p. 136.

The Spanish Economy in Profile

FIGURE III-2
Inflation in Spain: Percent Annual Variation of the Consumer Price Index

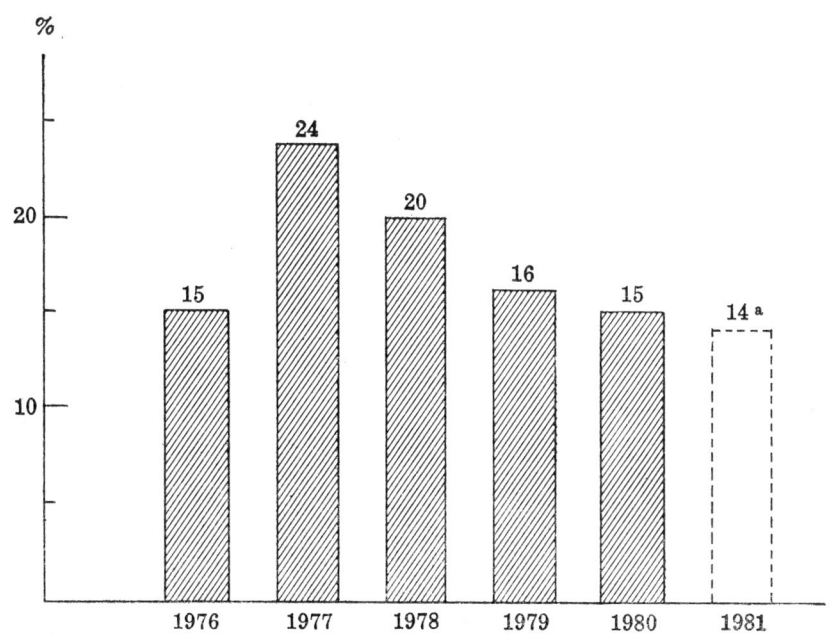

Year	%
1976	15
1977	24
1978	20
1979	16
1980	15
1981	14 [a]

Sources: Robert Graham, "Specter of unemployment grows as recession deepens," *Financial Times*, April 9, 1980, p. 2; and "Spain," *Business Europe*, February 6, 1981, p. 47.

[a] Projected.

resolve, however, and a decree issued in October 1977 effectively keeps almost all price controls in place.

> The October 1977 decree states that profit margins may not be increased and retained the "precios autorizados" [authorized prices] . . . and the "vigilanza especial" lists [now called "precios comunicados"]; the number of items on the first list has been reduced from 54 to 35, and on the second from 80 to 51.
>
> In addition, the government has set up a system by which provincial price councils will monitor the wholesaling and the retailing of perishable goods and supervise at the provincial level a small number of prices on both lists [only eight items in all, mainly public services]. The prices of all other goods and services are now freed.[56]

---

[56] "Spain," *Investing, Trading, and Licensing Conditions Abroad* (Business International Corporation, April 1978), p. 12.

Price increases must be authorized by the Council of Ministers, specifically by the Higher Price Council of the Ministry of Commerce, to which regulation power has been delegated. The Higher Price Council is aided by a number of special committees. For each major industrial sector and for each province additional price councils and committees have been set up.

The slow appreciation of the peseta due to the positive balance of payments and to increased foreign direct investment undoubtedly contributed to the easing of prices up to mid-1979. This trend, which followed the devaluation of the peseta in 1977 (see Figures III-3 and III-4), also caused a loss of competitiveness for Spanish goods and forced the balance of payments increasingly

FIGURE III-3

Price Competitiveness [a]

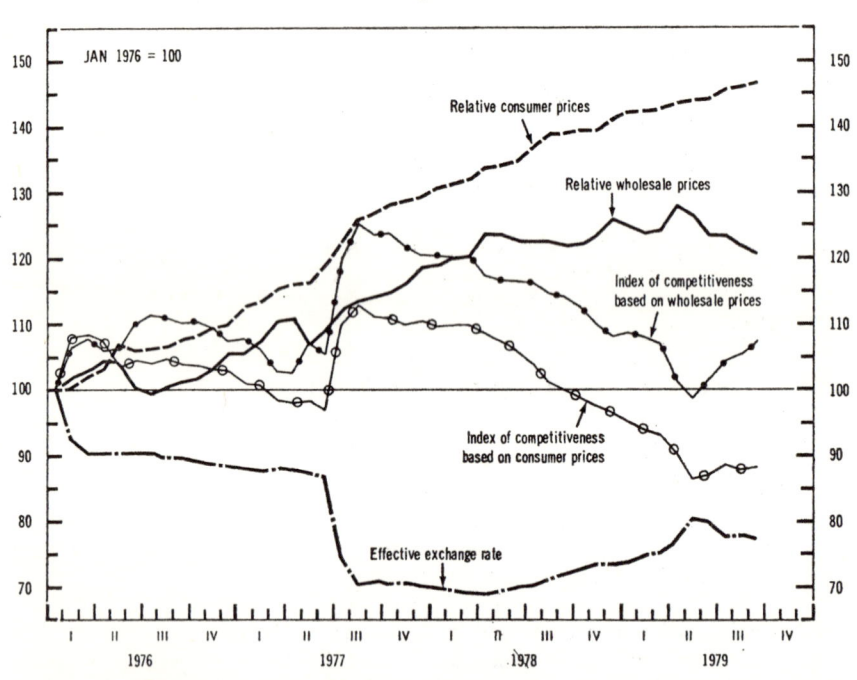

Source: Organisation for Economic Co-operation and Development, *OECD Economic Surveys: Spain* (Paris: OECD Publications, April 1980), p. 19.

[a] Relative prices are calculated as a ratio of prices in Spain to a trade-weighted average of prices in her 14 trading partners. Index of relative competitiveness is a product of relative prices and the effective exchange rate.

FIGURE III-4
Exchange Rate Developments

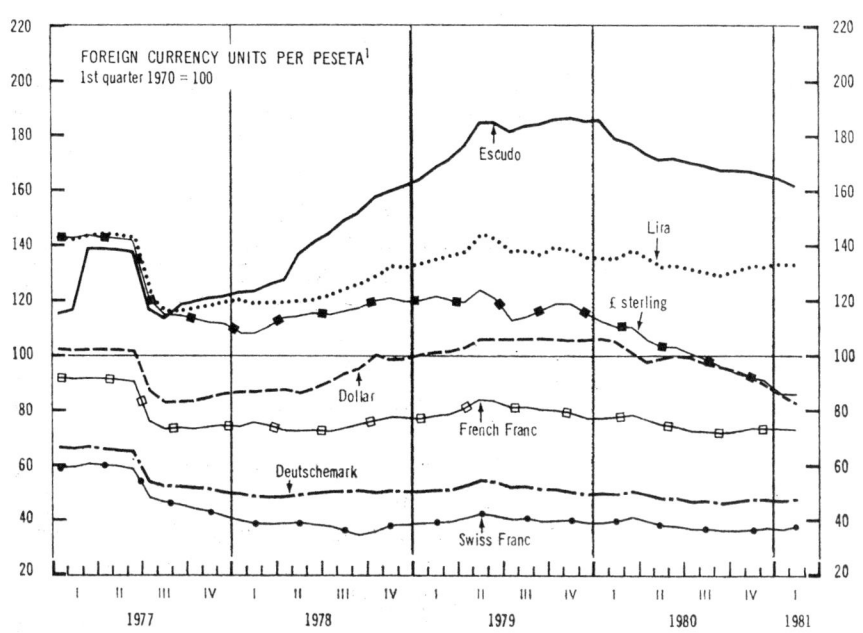

Source: Organisation for Economic Co-operation and Development, *OECD Economic Surveys: Spain* (Paris: OECD Publications, May 1981), p. 37.

[1] Monthly average of daily figures.

into the red for 1979. This, in turn, has caused the peseta to lose ground vis-à-vis other major currencies.

For 1980, the current account showed a deficit of about $5.0 billion. This caused a decrease in reserves of about $1 billion after a continuous rise which brought Spanish foreign reserves up to a so far unprecedented level of almost $13 million.

Spain's oil bill almost doubled from 1979 to 1980, amounting to $12 billion. This was one of the major factors in the weakening of the peseta, which started in the summer of 1980. The levelling off of dynamic exports that has characterized the Spanish economy since 1977 also helped the peseta's downward float, and businessmen have predicted a band between 97.00 and 98.00 pesetas per dollar at the 1981 basis.[57]

---

[57] Graham, "Better decision-making," p. III.

The Balance of Payments and Trade

For a time, the Spanish balance of payments showed a marked improvement over the disastrous year of 1976. The deficit of over $4 billion registered that year was largely because of the decision to "not [embark] on a national austerity plan"[58] following the great oil price hike of 1974. This had serious aftereffects, but the devaluation of the peseta, the Moncloa Pact, the stabilization of democracy with the subsequent passage of the National Energy Plan and the PEG all helped to bring about a return to the black in the current account balance by 1978, something which had not been registered since 1973. As has already been mentioned, however, the current account balance for 1980 again dropped and reached a record deficit of $5.0 billion. This development was mostly due to the doubling of the oil bill and to levelling off of the dynamic exports that characterized the Spanish economy.

The volume of merchandise exports expanded rapidly in 1978, while for the second consecutive year the volume of imports fell substantially. Low domestic demand and improved price competitiveness most likely are the major factors behind the favorable export performance in that year.[59]

"The balance of invisibles registered a record surplus of $5.5 billion in 1978. A major contribution was made by tourism, a net revenue of which rose by $1.4 billion to reach a record high of $4 billion."[60] A good harvest and a marked increase in hydro-energy production in 1979 also helped the situation, but most favorable conditions did not repeat themselves in 1980, and the balance of payments fell into the red.

Remittances from Spanish people working abroad, which usually provide some relief to the balance of payments, did not much help the situation. Although the remittances usually generate a large inflow of foreign currency, they did not increase by much since many more Spaniards now prefer to remain at home. (Table III-5 lists the balance of payments for selected years, while Table III-6 gives the foreign assets and liabilities of the various Spanish sectors and institutions.)

---

[58] *Situación*, April 1979, p. 18.

[59] *OECD Economic Surveys: Spain*, April 1979, pp. 15-16.

[60] *Ibid.*, p. 17.

TABLE III-5
Balance of Payments
(transactions basis, $ million)

	1976	1977	1978	1979	1980 [a]
Exports, FOB	8,991	10,611	13,480	18,352	20,004
Imports, FOB	16,318	16,832	17,505	24,022	31,949
Trade Balance	—7,328	—6,221	—4,024	—5,670	—11,945
Services (net)	1,891	2,620	3,974	5,014	4,850
Tourism	2,690	3,486	4,917	5,559	5,750
Investment Income	—502	—760	—1,109	—1,088	—1,500
Technical Assistance and Royalties	—406	—328	—325	—403	—486
Transfers (net)	1,142	1,151	1,656	1,782	2,000
Current Balance	—4,294	—2,450	1,606	1,126	—5,095
Long-term Capital, Net	1,920	3,219	1,495	3,010	3,805
Official	571	1,259	—461	346	395
Private	1,350	1,960	1,956	2,664	3,410
Foreign Capital to Spain			2,871	3,370	4,600
Investments			1,221	1,498	1,500
Loans, Credits, Others			1,650	1,872	3,100
Spanish Capital to Foreign Countries			—915	—706	—1,190
Basic Balance	—2,374	769	3,101	4,136	—1,290
Short-term Capital [b]	1,256	144	736	—735	434

TABLE III-5 (continued)

Balance on Non-Monetary Transactions	−1,117	914	3,837	3,402	−856
Monetary Transaction	86	231	−95	25	140
IMF Oil Facility	88			−512	
SDR				70	76
Change in Official Reserves	−943	1,145	3,743	2,985	−640
Memorandum Item[a]:					
Oil Imports	4,290	4,364	4,529	6,667	11,919
Non-oil Imports	12,028	12,468	12,976	17,355	20,030
Non-oil Trade Balance	−3,037	−1,857	505	997	−26

Source: Organisation for Economic Co-operation and Development, *OECD Economic Surveys: Spain* (Paris: OECD Publications, May 1981), p. 36.
[a] Provisional secretariat estimates.
[b] Including errors and omissions, and banks' internal foreign exchange accounts.

TABLE III-6
Foreign Assets and Liabilities
(outstanding at end of period, $ billions)

	1973	1974	1975	1976	1977	1978	1979	September 1980
LIABILITIES	11.6	14.3	17.3	21.0	27.0	33.4	41.2	47.6
Monetary Institutions	5.1	5.7	7.5	9.1	11.6	15.7	21.0	24.0
Bank of Spain [a,b]	0.1	0.1	0.7	0.8	0.8	0.9	0.4	0.5
Banking System [a,c]	5.0	5.6	6.8	8.3	10.8	14.8	20.6	23.5
Government [b,d]	0.4	0.2	0.3	0.7	1.6	0.7	0.1	—0.3
Private Sector	6.1	8.4	9.5	11.2	13.8	17.0	20.1	23.9
Short-term Credits (net) [b,c]	0.1	0.0	0.1	0.0	0.6	0.9	0.9	1.3
Long-term Credits [b,d]	3.1	4.7	5.1	6.5	7.8	9.5	11.1	13.4
Foreign Investment [b,e]	2.9	3.7	4.3	4.7	5.4	6.6	8.1	9.2
ASSETS	—11.3	—10.5	—10.7	—11.0	—13.7	—21.8	—28.7	—30.6
Monetary Institutions	—10.7	—9.7	—9.6	—9.5	—12.9	—19.5	—26.1	—27.5
Bank of Spain [a]	—6.9	—6.7	—6.4	—5.7	—6.8	—11.2	—14.2	—13.7
Reserves	—6.8	—6.5	—6.1	—5.4	—6.6	—10.7	—13.8	—13.4
Gold [f]	(—0.6)	(—0.6)	(—0.6)	(—0.6)	(—0.6)	(—0.6)	(—0.6)	(—0.6)
Foreign Exchange [c]	(—6.2)	(—5.9)	(—5.5)	(—4.8)	(—6.0)	(—10.1)	(—13.2)	(—12.8)
Other [b]	—0.1	—0.2	—0.3	—0.3	—0.2	—0.5	—0.4	—0.3
Banking System [a,c]	—3.8	—3.0	—3.2	—3.8	—5.1	—8.3	—11.9	—13.8
Government [b,c]	—0.2	—0.2	—0.2	—0.3	—0.2	—0.5	—0.6	—0.5

TABLE III-6 (continued)

Private Sector	−0.4	−0.6	−0.9	−1.3	−1.5	−1.7	−2.0	−2.6
Long-term Credits [b,e]	−0.3	−0.3	−0.5	−0.6	−0.6	−0.6	−0.6	−0.6
Investments Abroad [b,e]	−0.1	−0.3	−0.4	−0.7	−0.9	−1.1	−1.4	−2.0

Source: Organisation for Economic Co-operation and Development, *OECD Economic Surveys: Spain* (Paris: OECD Publications, May 1981), p. 59.

[a] Balance-sheet items.
[b] Item valued at then prevailing historical exchange rates.
[c] Item valued at end-of-period exchange rate.
[d] Official foreign debt estimates, based on exchange control records.
[e] Estimate obtained by adding up balance of payments flows from 1969 onward.
[f] Valued at U.S. $42.22 per ounce.

The Spanish Economy in Profile

In 1979, Spain's major trading partners were the EEC, the Latin American Free Trade Association (LAFTA), the United States, the European Free Trade Association (EFTA), and the Council for Mutual Economic Assistance (COMECON). The trade balance in the late seventies turned into a surplus in free on board (FOB) terms because exports tended to rise faster than imports in exchanges both with the EEC and with the COMECON countries. This was true despite the "self limitations" of exports forced on Spain by the EEC in sectors such as textiles and steel, as well as the already discussed loss of competitiveness of Spanish goods due to the upward floating of the peseta. "On the other hand, trade with EFTA countries deteriorated with respect to 1978, underlining the need to put into effect as soon as possible the preferential trade Agreement signed last year [1978] by Spain and EFTA." [61] (See Tables III-7 and III-8 for an overview of Spain's major trading partners and major imports and exports, respectively.)

Spain's trade with the EEC dwarfs in importance trade with any other country or area. Thus, it is of crucial importance to Spain to continue negotiations for EEC membership. These negotiations have recently become increasingly difficult, and the entry of Spain into the EEC, originally planned for 1981 (together with Greece), now seems to have been delayed almost indefinitely. Strong opposition to Spain's membership from France, different opinions as to the pace of tariff dismantling by Spain (which Spaniards claim should not be too fast so that industry is not damaged by the sudden removal of the protection it has enjoyed until now), problems over a common agricultural policy (France and Italy are afraid cheap Spanish agricultural products may swamp the market) and over the free movement of workers are all obstacles which cannot easily be removed. The recent coup, however, provided Spain with an added incentive to do all that is necessary to join the EEC quickly, since it is believed that Common Market membership will be a consolidating factor for its new democracy.

In order to join the EEC, Spain will need to dismantle the tariffs existing between it and the EEC and to adopt the Common Foreign Tariff (CFT) which is applied to Third World countries. The CFT is much lower than the tariff presently

---

[61] *Economic Report 1979*, p. 54.

TABLE III-7
Spain's Foreign Trade, by Tariff Sections
(in millions of pesetas)

	Imports 1978	Imports 1979	1979-78 (%)	Exports 1978	Exports 1979	1979-78 (%)	Import Coverage 1978	Import Coverage 1979
Animals and Animal Products	39,591	59,263	142	18,614	24,584	132	47.0	41.5
Vegetable Products	135,632	135,300	98	90,952	121,494	134	67.1	89.8
Fats and Oils	11,235	10,354	92	22,279	27,275	122	198.3	263.4
Food Products	55,940	54,655	98	71,065	80,761	114	127.0	147.8
Mineral Products	453,421	564,714	124	58,405	61,675	105	12.9	10.9
Chemical Products	124,452	148,600	119	57,629	75,990	132	46.3	51.1
Plastic Materials, Rubber	37,407	47,884	128	39,006	48,617	125	104.3	101.5
Furs, Leather, Rubber	23,402	28,264	121	19,196	24,615	128	82.0	87.1
Timber and Cork	25,303	28,935	114	13,973	16,807	121	54.8	58.1
Cellulose, Paper and By-products	25,609	31,689	124	35,428	45,803	129	138.3	144.5
Textile Materials and Products	40,726	50,148	123	58,808	63,874	109	144.4	127.4
Footwear, etc.	1,968	3,245	165	46,769	48,554	104	2,376.5	1,496.3
Plaster, Stone Products, etc.	15,517	18,868	122	20,777	24,835	119	133.9	131.6
Fine Pearls, etc.	24,175	26,129	108	7,100	8,755	123	29.4	33.5
Basic Metals	85,439	113,842	133	158,318	194,677	123	185.3	171.0
Machinery, Electrical Equipment	214,388	233,694	109	118,974	154,145	130	55.5	66.0
Transport Equipment	53,373	78,561	147	135,159	166,415	123	253.2	211.8
Scientific Instruments, etc.	52,160	56,391	108	6,778	8,997	133	13.0	15.9
Arms and Ammunition	758	887	117	3,296	3,570	108	434.8	402.5
Miscellaneous	8,177	11,127	136	18,511	19,457	105	226.4	174.9
Objets d'Art	2,369	1,471	62	447	639	143	18.9	43.4
	1,431,033	1,704,022	119	1,001,383	1,221,441	122	70.0	71.7

Source: *Economic Report 1979* (annual publication released by the Banco de Bilbao), p. 53.

TABLE III-8
Foreign Trade by Geographical Area
(in billions of pesetas)

	Imports, CIF					Exports, FOB				
	1976	1977	1978	1979	1980	1976	1977	1978	1979	1980
EEC, total	380.3	461.4	496.3	606.2	739.5	271.3	358.8	457.8	586.2	723.6
United Kingdom	56.3	71.3	77.6	87.8	115.1	42.3	49.0	58.7	87.6	105.3
France	91.3	113.1	130.1	164.7	202.4	84.8	123.6	166.4	197.0	246.6
Germany	116.9	136.2	142.4	163.2	200.8	63.8	82.0	106.8	126.2	152.9
Italy	54.8	68.2	67.5	90.1	120.9	24.5	39.4	49.9	78.8	116.7
COMECON	28.8	26.3	29.0	37.9	55.2	20.0	21.7	27.1	36.7	39.1
Other European Countries	77.4	74.3	78.9	98.8	128.6	60.3	71.9	95.1	103.6	143.6
United States	165.9	162.0	190.1	211.7	318.8	59.6	76.1	92.8	85.1	79.4
Canada	10.5	11.7	11.5	15.9	19.4	6.8	7.6	8.8	10.4	10.6
Other American Countries	82.6	121.9	119.3	152.5	231.0	57.3	79.4	96.0	136.7	159.1
Japan	45.1	43.0	40.1	39.9	60.5	9.3	8.9	15.2	24.6	19.2
Near East	242.1	257.7	250.6	288.1	530.8	19.1	24.2	45.6	49.8	100.1
Rest of the World	137.7	192.3	215.6	253.0	366.9	79.8	126.8	163.1	188.0	218.5
Total	1,170.4	1,350.5	1,431.6	1,704.0	2,450.7	583.5	775.3	1,001.6	1,221.2	1,493.2

Source: Organisation for Economic Co-operation and Development, *OECD Economic Surveys: Spain* (Paris: OECD Publications, May 1981), p. 58.

applied by Spain to non-EEC members.[62] This liberalization of the Spanish frontiers will bring about a serious imbalance in the Spanish economy, but the long transition period (ten years) and the more open market economy will hopefully reap more benefits than damages.

WAGES, UNEMPLOYMENT, AND THE JOB MARKET

Although the overall labor force participation rate decreased from 51.2 percent in 1974 to 48.5 percent in 1978, unemployment kept rising, and the trend is expected to continue in the 1980s. It presently stands at a record 11 percent, or 1.5 million workers.[63] This is indeed one of the major problems facing Spain today, and the governmental measures designed to prevent layoffs and to help youth find jobs seem to have provided little help.[64] In fact, experts predict that unemployment will continue to rise. Youth unemployment presents the most distressing statistics in the matter. At the end of 1978, there were 21.1 percent young people unemployed, aged between fifteen and twenty-five. The unemployment rate for women was also rather high, reaching 8.9 percent in 1978. This may be largely due to the current social trend of more and more women joining the labor ranks.[65]

On the basis of the many analyses made by several institutions, it can be concluded that the unemployment situation cannot be solved by increasing the rate of growth of economic activity. New investments do not always produce an increase in employment, and sometimes even decrease it. (See Figure III-5 for a graphical illustration of the upward surge in unemployment.)

> Besides the traditional measures in stimulation policies directed to the creating of new jobs, consideration is now being given to the redistribution or reallocation of the demand for existing labour amongst all suppliers of the same; it will be necessary to reorganise practices as prevalent as overtime and the holding of more than one job and even reduction of the working day in order for there to be jobs for everyone. Clearly this also involves a redistribution of income within an economy of greater austerity.[66]

---

[62] *Informe Económico 1979*, p. 166.

[63] Robert Graham, "Rise in Spanish unemployment to over 11%," *Financial Times*, August 7, 1980, p. 2.

[64] *OECD Economic Surveys: Spain*, April 1979, pp. 10-11.

[65] *Economic Report 1978*, p. 52.

[66] *Ibid.*, p. 55.

The Spanish Economy in Profile

FIGURE III-5
Trend of Unemployment

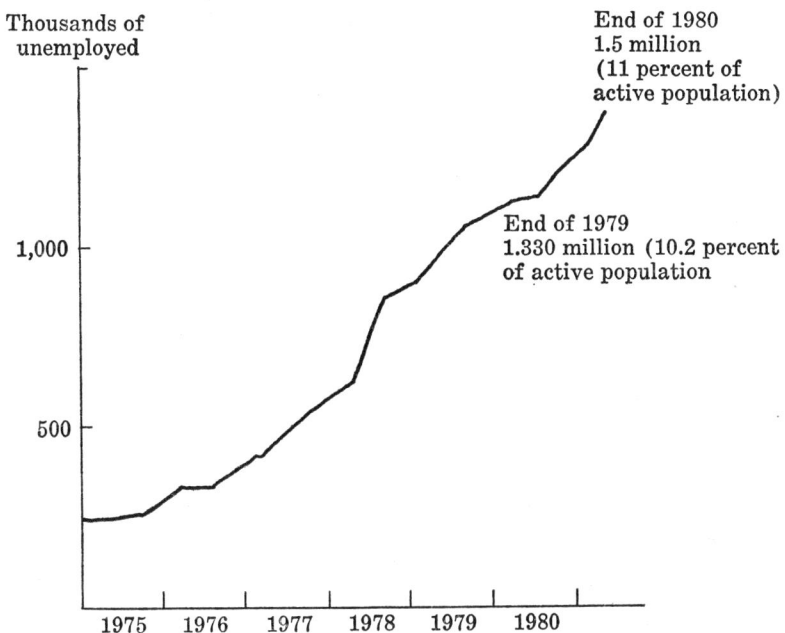

[Chart showing unemployment trend from 1975 to 1980, with y-axis "Thousands of unemployed" marked at 500 and 1,000. Annotations: "End of 1980 1.5 million (11 percent of active population)" and "End of 1979 1.330 million (10.2 percent of active population"]

Sources: *Informe Económico 1978* (annual publication released by the Banco de Bilbao), p. 141; *Informe Económico 1979*, p. 144; Robert Graham, "Spectre of unemployment grows as recession deepens," *Financial Times*, April 9, 1980, p. 2; Robert Graham, "Rise in Spanish unemployment to over 11%," *Financial Times*, August 7, p. 2.

Table III-9 shows the structure and the trends of the Spanish labor market. The data indicate that Spain is progressively moving away from an agricultural society to an industrialized and services-oriented one. This may also be one of the primary reasons for the enormous increase in unemployment. Another important factor contributing to the skyrocketing number of the jobless is the lack of emigration by Spaniards. The trend of high emigration in the early sixties has apparently disappeared completely; since the mid-seventies, considerable numbers of Spanish people working abroad have been returning home. Less and less workers are willing to leave home and family to look for fortune abroad, and many more are deciding to return to their country of origin. This trend, which is also being set in Italy, seems to point out that, notwithstanding the economic problems and the inflation rate, there is a rising prosperity that allows for more people to reenter the country. The sense of despair that

TABLE III-9
Labor Market Trends

	1977	1978	1979	1980	1980 1st Quarter	1980 2nd Quarter	1980 3rd Quarter[c]	1980 4th Quarter
	(in thousands)							
Civilian Labor Force [a]	13,172	13,172	13,101	12,954	13,117	13,004	12,836	12,860
Civilian Employment [a]	12,423	12,181	11,896	11,426	11,646	11,477	11,341	11,240
Agriculture	2,568[b]	2,495	2,343	2,159	2,251	2,153	2,114	2,119
Industry	3,432[b]	3,359	3,251	3,109	3,176	3,105	3,096	3,057
Construction	1,243[b]	1,175	1,109	1,028	1,045	1,056	1,027	984
Services	5,172[b]	5,152	5,194	5,131	5,174	5,163	5,105	5,080
Employees (total)	8,746	8,580	8,356	8,005	8,201	8,042	7,921	7,855
Unemployment	749	991	1,205	1,528	1,471	1,527	1,495	1,620
	(percent)							
Participation Rate (total)	48.9	48.3	47.7	47.9	47.5	46.9	48.5	48.5
Men	72.5	71.3	70.4	70.7	69.8	69.2	72.0	71.7
Women	27.1	27.0	26.7	26.8	26.8	26.2	26.9	27.1
Unemployment Rate (total)	5.7	7.5	9.2	11.7	11.2	11.7	11.6	12.6
Men	5.4	7.0	8.7	11.2	10.6	11.2	11.0	11.9
Women	6.3	8.8	10.5	13.3	12.6	13.0	13.3	14.3
Less than 25 Years Old	15.8	19.0	23.0	29.4	27.2	29.0	29.5	31.8
25-54 Years Old	3.5	4.4	5.5	7.3	7.0	7.2	7.2	7.8
Over 55 Years Old	2.4	2.9	3.5	4.5	4.3	4.6	4.4	4.7

Source: Organisation for Economic Co-operation and Development, *OECD Economic Surveys: Spain* (Paris: OECD Publications, May 1981), p. 52.
[a] These include the professional military but exclude those who are on compulsory military services.
[b] Average of last two quarters only.
[c] As from third quarter 1980, labor force excludes population aged between 14 and 15 years.

The Spanish Economy in Profile 57

forced people to emigrate is no longer there and hopefully will never return to Spain. (Table III-10 shows the trend of Spanish emigration for the years 1961 to 1978.)

TABLE III-10
Spanish Emigration, Europe and Overseas: 1961-1978

	Leaving	Returning[a]	Migratory balance
1961	115,372	7,815	107,557
1962	142,505	45,844	96,661
1963	134,541	52,230	82,311
1964	192,999	112,871	80,128
1965	181,278	120,678	60,600
1966	141,997	143,082	— 1,085
1967	60,000	85,000	—25,000
1968	85,662	67,622	18,000
1969	112,205	43,336	68,869
1970	105,538	40,000	65,674
1971	120,984	50,000	70,348
1972	110,431	70,000	40,369
1973	100,927	110,000	— 9,073
1974	55,464	140,000	—84,473
1975	24,515	70,000	—45,485
1976	15,642	70,000	—54,358
1977	14,957	60,000	—45,053
1978[b]	15,227	40,000	—24,773

Source: *Economic Report 1978* (annual publication released by the Banco de Bilbao), p. 56.
[a] Estimates.
[b] Information until the month of November.

Notwithstanding that there are many difficulties in interpreting the data and that the statistics are often incomplete and inexact, it can certainly be said that Spain has undergone a tremendous transformation. The Spanish people have decreased their birth rate, are enjoying a higher standard of living, and generally seem to have improved their lot considerably since the 1950s. This is primarily due to improved resource allocation, to the international transfer of modern mechanical and managerial methods, greater competitiveness, an enormous increase in the quantity of equipment, and a large increase in foreign investment.[67] After the accelerated growth of the boom years between 1960 and 1974, however, real Spanish income fell to modest increases that barely exceed population growth.[68] (Tables III-11 and III-12 provide a good review of the income distribution and evolution in Spain.)

[67] *Informe Económico 1979*, p. 271.
[68] *Economic Report 1978*, p. 21.

TABLE III-11
General Indicator of Economic Activity and Social Welfare [a]

	1967	1968	1969	1970	1971	1972	1973
Working Population (% annual change)	0.98	0.93	0.58	1.11	1.04	1.32	2.05
Unemployment (in thousands)	231.1	240.1	182.8	192.9	256.0	391.5	361.8
Balance of Payments Current Account (in millions of dollars)	−456	−242	−394	78	856	571	557
Gini Index, Personal Distribution of Income	0.463	0.461	0.459	0.457	0.454	0.451	0.449
Increase in Cost of Living (average yearly rate)	6.4	4.9	2.2	5.7	8.2	8.3	11.4
Real Increase in Average Annual Salaries	7.7	2.8	10.2	5.6	4.1	6.1	5.4
GDP Growth Rate	5.5	6.5	8.4	5.9	4.9	8.4	8.5
Rate of Investment Increase	12.5	8.7	11.2	6.2	−2.9	15.9	14.3
Rate of Increase in Household Consumption	5.6	4.3	6.5	4.1	4.8	8.2	8.1

	1974	1975	1976	1977	1978	1979
Working Population (% annual change)	0.64	−0.70	−0.84	0.43	−0.47	−0.07
Unemployment (in thousands)	431.4	619.7	730.1	831.8	1,083.2	1,334.2
Balance of Payments Current Account (in millions of dollars)	−3,278	−3,477	−4,300	−2,512	+1,400	+400
Gini Index, Personal Distribution of Income	0.446	0.442	0.438	0.429	0.423	0.420
Increase in Cost of Living (average yearly rate)	15.7	17.0	17.7	24.6	19.8	15.7
Real Increase in Average Annual Salaries	7.4	6.8	5.2	2.1	5.1	1.6
GDP Growth Rate	5.4	1.1	2.9	2.6	3.1	1.4
Rate of Investment Increase	6.7	−3.9	−2.0	−1.2	−4.7	−1.9
Rate of Increase in Household Consumption	5.8	3.0	−5.0	1.0	2.5	1.8

Source: *Economic Report 1979* (annual publication released by the Banco de Bilbao), p. 22.

[a] Basic data used.

TABLE III-12
*Structure and Evolution of National Income,
Gross Domestic Product and Production Factors*

	% Change over the Previous Year				% of GDP		
	1974	1978	1979	1974	1978	1979	
National Income (at factor cost)	23.0	23.4	16.7	91.71	90.19	88.91
Gross Domestic Product (at factor cost)	23.1	24.0	17.4	100.00	100.00	100.00
Earned Income	26.5	23.7	16.3	54.91	58.43	57.90
Wages and Salaries	27.1	23.4	15.3	44.99	45.93	45.13
Social Security Contributions	23.9	24.8	19.9	9.92	12.49	12.76
Gross Operating Surplus	19.1	24.4	18.9	45.09	41.57	42.10
Depreciation	27.8	28.2	32.8	8.51	9.07	10.27
Net Operating Surplus	17.3	23.4	15.0	36.58	32.50	31.84
Other Income	17.6	21.3	11.9	20.67	18.99	18.10
Farming Income	2.3	22.5	5.0	5.78	5.35	4.78
Income of Traders, Businessmen, and Members of the Professions	24.8	20.8	14.6	14.89	13.64	13.32
Public Sector Income	22.2	31.0	20.1	2.82	3.35	3.43
Unearned Income	15.8	25.1	19.0	13.08	10.17	10.31
Interest and Dividends	6.3	29.3	25.6	3.94	2.98	3.19
Retained Profits of Companies and Businesses	22.4	25.1	18.1	4.61	3.08	3.10
Letting Income	18.5	22.4	14.9	4.53	4.11	4.02

Source: *Economic Report 1979* (annual publication released by the Banco de Bilbao), p. 20.

60   *Spain*

As noted before, the Moncloa Pact helped contain wage hikes in 1978 to 22 percent. In 1979, wage increases were held down to just under 15 percent, perhaps because of the easing of inflation and because of the UGT-CEOE pact signed in 1979—which was not, however, adhered to by the largest trade union, the CCOO. The same was true for 1980. (Figure III-6 gives an idea of wage and price trends for a quick comparison.)

FIGURE III-6
Price and Wage Developments
(percentage change from corresponding quarter of previous year)

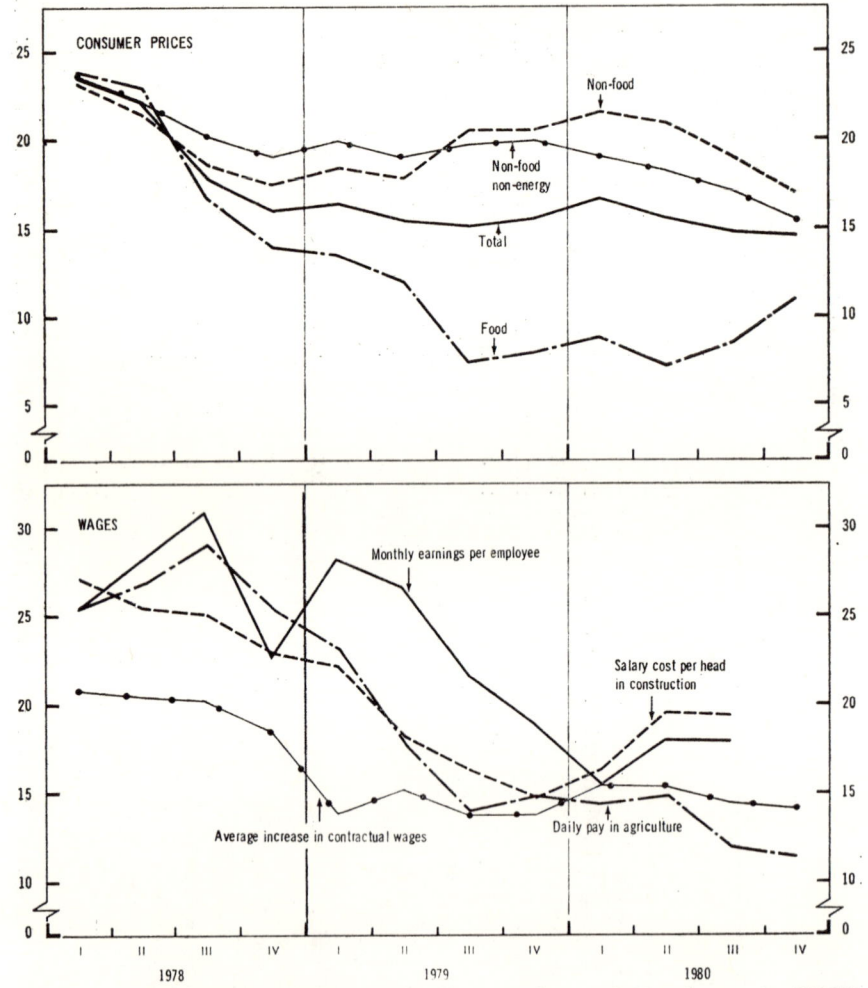

Source: Organisation for Economic Co-operation and Development, *OECD Economic Surveys: Spain* (Paris: OECD Publications, May 1981), p. 34.

The Spanish Economy in Profile

The legal minimum daily wage (MDW) was set at 640 pesetas in 1979, or 18,000 pesetas per month (gross amount). Table III-13 shows how the MDW has increased in the seventies and

TABLE III-13
Minimum Daily Pay

Year	Minimum Daily Pay (pesetas)	Percent of Basic Needs
1970	120	37
1975	280	44
1976	345	45
April 1977	440	—
August 1978	600	—
September 1979	640	—

Sources: European Trade Union Institute, *Enlargement of the EC following the Accession of Greece, Spain and Portugal: Socio-Economic Aspects* (Brussels: ETUI, 1979), p. 68; "Spain," *Business Europe*, April 15, 1979, p. 142.

what percentage of the basic needs it covers, according to the European Trade Union Institute. Table III-14 gives the average wages for salaried workers in Spanish industry.

It is difficult to judge salaries in comparison to other countries, especially if the salaries are not the current ones due to a publication delay by the Spanish Statistical Institute. Therefore, in an attempt to convey how Spanish workers fare against workers from other industrialized and less industrialized countries, Table III-15 gives the estimated hourly compensation of production workers around the world.

Even though salaries have risen considerably in the post-Franco years, the hourly compensation to Spanish workers is only about 66 percent that of American workers. Moreover, additional compensation to workers is only 40 percent of their hourly earnings. This is a rather low level, similar to that existing in the United States, and considerably lower than that in neighboring European countries such as France or Italy, where the ratios are 80.6 and 96 percent, respectively.

It is interesting to note how well Spain's economic performance fares against other industrialized and less industrialized

TABLE III-14
Average Wages for Spanish Workers

	Average Pay in Pts/hr			
	Blue-Collar Workers		White-Collar Workers	
Type of Activity	1978	1979	1978	1979
Extraction and Preparation of Solid Fuels	258.64	303.47	489.96	554.79
Electricity, Gas and Water	277.54	340.17	534.52	672.84
Extraction and Preparation of Metallic Minerals	216.11	322.60	433.82	627.77
Chemical Industries	242.90	318.39	460.91	658.21
Manufacturing of Metal Products (except Machines and Autos)	237.67	328.09	375.41	492.47
Manufacturing of Office Machines and Electronic Materials	267.16	334.18	471.88	579.98
Automotive Industry	284.90	367.48	484.39	575.92
Food and Tobacco Industry	211.89	267.56	376.21	512.18
Textile Industry	198.02	256.96	349.44	455.24
Leather and Shoe Industry	176.88	238.18	284.32	424.66
Wood Industry	181.78	230.61	277.90	431.86
Paper Industry	233.65	307.64	434.76	592.96
Graphic Arts and Printing	250.60	342.70	399.84	539.83
Rubber and Plastics	205.40	277.52	437.10	508.20
Construction	216.73	263.26	403.27	571.86
Hotels and Restaurants	138.31	180.45	269.13	415.01
Financial Institutions	274.77	349.78	575.14	750.27
Insurance	225.17	324.63	657.24	563.78

Sources: Ministerio de Economía, *España 1979: Anuario Estadístico* (Madrid: Instituto Nacional de Estadística, 1979), p. 313; *ibid., España 1980.*

countries. Looking at Table III-16, we see that Spain's per capita GDP is close to that of Italy and far ahead that of countries such as Turkey. The inflation rate, though still high, has moved within the margin of other industrialized countries. The unemployment rate, however, is alarming and gives no sign of decreasing. Productivity growth has kept up with other industrialized nations, but it is hoped that it will increase at a higher rate in the future, as Spain needs to "catch up" with the EEC countries, an arduous task at best. Enormous progress has been made, but there is yet a long way to go, especially

TABLE III-15
Estimated Hourly Compensation of Production Workers in Manufacturing: Thirteen Countries, Mid-Year 1980 [a]

Country	Exchange Rate [b] National Currency Unit	Exchange Rate [b] National Currency Units per U.S. Dollar	Average Hourly Earnings in National Currency	Ratio of Additional Compensation to Hourly Earnings	Hourly Compensation National Currency	Hourly Compensation U.S. Dollars	Hourly Compensation Index U.S.=100
United States	Dollar	—	7.25	36.4	9.89	9.89	100
Canada	Dollar	1.164	8.14	26.0	10.26	8.81	89
Mexico	Peso	22.91	48.17	33.4	64.26	2.80	28
Japan	Yen	231.1	1,100	20.0 [c]	1,320	5.71	58
Korea [d]	Won	603.0 [e]	563	15-20	662 [f]	1.10	11
Belgium	Franc	28.75	223.3	72.4	385.0	13.39	135
France	Franc	4.159	22.17	80.6	40.04	9.63	97
Germany	Mark	1.786	13.33	63.3	21.77	12.19	123
Italy	Lira	839.3	3,885	96.0	7,615	9.07	92
Netherlands	Guilder	1.958	13.92	73.6 [c]	24.17	12.34	125
Spain	Peseta	70.07	329 [g]	40.0	460	6.57	66
Sweden	Krona	4.200	32.20	62.7	52.39	12.46	126
United Kingdom	Pence	43.37	236.0	29.7	306.1	7.06	71

Source: U.S. Department of Labor, Bureau of Labor Statistics, Office of Productivity and Technology, November 1980.

[a] Provisional estimates.
[b] January-September average except for Korea.
[c] All employees.
[d] Earnings for production workers estimated on the basis of average hourly earnings for all employees, adjusted for the relative level of production worker earnings to all employee earnings in 1977.
[e] June exchange rate.
[f] Mid-point of estimated average compensation range.
[g] Earnings are estimated on the basis of 1978 manufacturing earnings and the average earnings trend in the total private nonfarm economy since 1978.

TABLE III-16
International Comparisons:
1979

Country	1980 Per Capita GDP ($)	Inflation Rate	Productivity Growth	Unemployment (% of working population)
United States	9,602	8.0	n.a.	8.0
West Germany	10,626	4.8	2.6 [b]	4.0
France	8,827	10.7	2.6 [b]	8.0
Great Britain	5,514	16.1	2.6 [b]	6.5
Spain	3,967	18.8	2.7 [c]	9.5
Turkey	1,129	30.0 [a]	n.a.	n.a.
Greece	3,355	15.5	4.9 [c]	4.0
Portugal	1,864	19.8	5.4 [c]	n.a.
Italy	4,180	17.0	2.6 [b]	8.0 [d]

Sources: Organisation for Economic Co-operation and Development, "Basic Studies: International Comparisons," *OECD Economic Surveys: Spain* (Paris: OECD Publications, April 1980); European Trade Union Institute, *Enlargement of the EC following the Accession of Greece, Spain and Portugal: Socio-Economic Aspect* (Brussels: ETUI, 1979); "Spain," *Business Europe*, January 4, 1980, pp. 4-5.
[a] 1972 to 1977.
[b] EEC average before entry of Greece.
[c] 1970 to 1975.
n.a. = not available.

given the increasing economic difficulties that all industrialized nations will have to face in the years to come.

More important still in conditioning economic developments over the coming year will be the posture of the Government. In his speech to Parliament, seeking a vote of confidence in September, Sr. Suarez put the economy as a top priority. In over four years of talking about the priority nature of the economy, this was the first formal gesture underlining such a commitment. In the past, the Government has always become side-tracked by political issues. There are already indications of this. If this proves the case, the current economic team, which deserves a measure of confidence, will be quickly discredited.[69]

THE ROLE OF THE STATE

The Spanish government participates actively, for one reason or another, in many economic sectors. Radio, television, the railroad system, and Iberia—the national airline—are all owned and operated by the government. A large portion of public holdings is administered through the Instituto Nacional de Industria

---
[69] Graham, "Better decision-making," p. III.

(INI), an autonomous public institution. It was founded by Generalissimo Francisco Franco after the Civil War to help rebuild Spain and is modeled after the Italian Institute for Industrial Reconstruction, also founded by a dictator, Benito Mussolini. INI has both direct and indirect holdings in the industrial and service sectors.

> At the end of 1978, INI held direct, and in some cases majority, participation in 70 different firms (and indirect participation in over 200) with an invested capital of $13.2 billion and 260,000 employees. Its industrial activities are widely diversified and account for the following percentages of national production: 15 percent of electricity generated, 35 percent of automobile and 30 percent of industrial vehicle manufacturing, 65 percent of petroleum refined, 60 percent of steel production, 50 percent of coal mined and 95 percent of ship construction. INI also has large holdings in service industries such as air transport, tourism, regional development, banks, foreign trade and in the development of new technology.[70]

Table III-17 lists the major industrial companies with the relative government share, while Figure III-7 gives an idea of

TABLE III-17
INI's Major Industrial Companies

Company	Product	Government Share (%)	Foreign Shareholdings (%)
ENSIDESA [a]	Iron and Steel	88.7	—
Empresa Nacional del Petroleo (ENPETROL) [b]	Oil Refineries, Chemicals, Fertilizers	71.8	22.0
CASA	Aircraft Repairs and Production	65.6	24.5
Minas de Almagrera	Lead and Pyrites Mining	95.6	—
Potasas de Navarra	Potash Mining	100.0	—
ENASA	Trucks	67.2	—
ENDASA	Aluminum Smelters	54.4	25.0
ENCE	Pulp and Paper	81.0	—
IGFISA	Cold Storage	75.0	—
Bazan	Shipbuilding	100.0	—

Source: "Spain," *Investing, Licensing and Trading Conditions Abroad* (Business International Corporation, 1970), p. 5.
[a] Has absorbed Unisa.
[b] ENPETROL resulted from the merger of three former oil-refining companies: ENCASO, REPESA, and ENTASA.

---

[70] U.S. Department of Commerce, *Marketing in Spain* (Washington, D.C.: U.S. Government Printing Office, 1979), p. 5.

FIGURE III-7
Spanish Public Sector Holdings

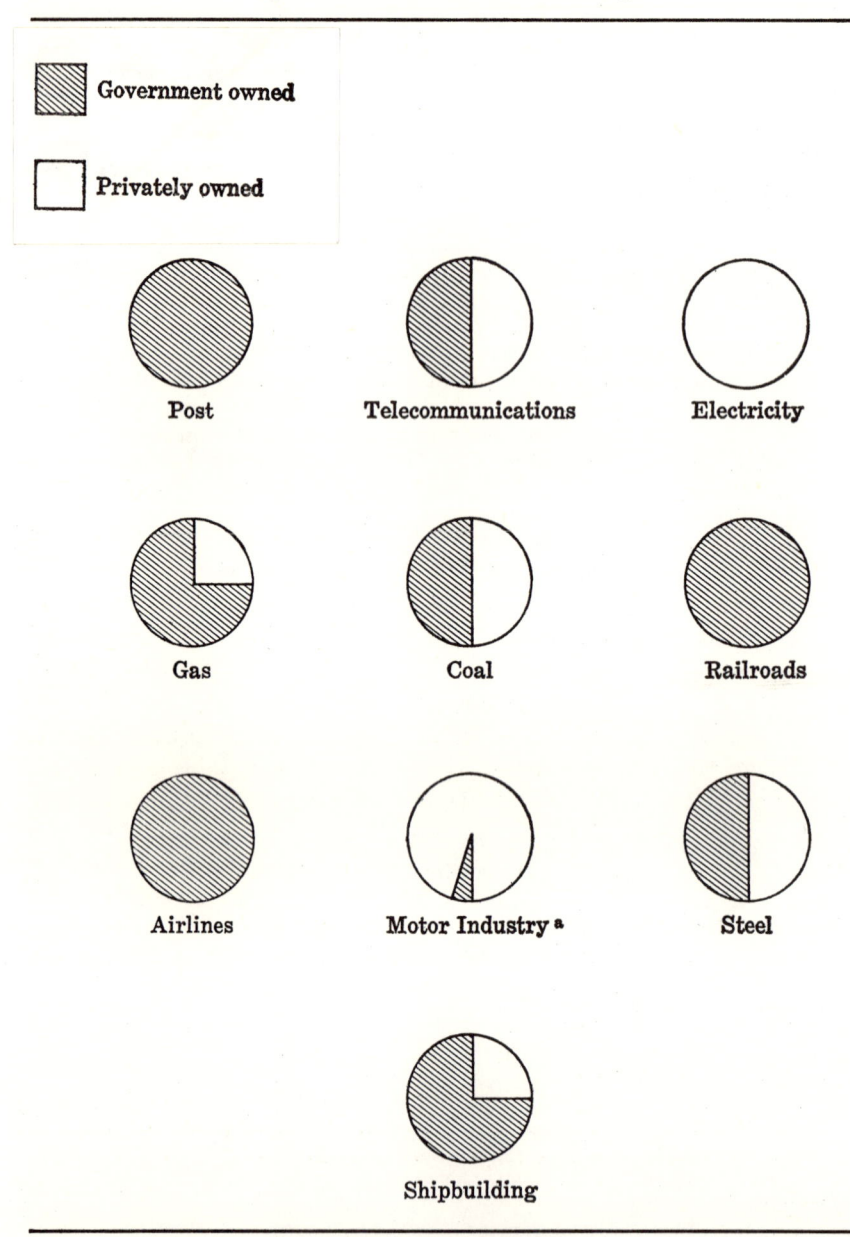

▨ Government owned

☐ Privately owned

Post

Telecommunications

Electricity

Gas

Coal

Railroads

Airlines

Motor Industry [a]

Steel

Shipbuilding

Source: "The State in the Market," *The Economist*, December 30, 1978, p. 39.

[a] *The Economist* lists the Spanish motor industry as totally private. It is well known, however, that INI owns 66.6 percent of Enasa, a truck manufacturing company, and that it owned about one-third of SEAT.

the government shareholdings in different sectors of industry.

To get an idea of just how large INI really is, it suffices to say that more than 10 percent of the total gross industrial product of Spain was attributable to its subsidiaries and affiliated firms in 1978.[71] "INI was founded by the Franco regime [in 1961] in order to create industries that would contribute to national defence and self-sufficiency and in order to provide lifebelts for sinking ducks .... INI prides itself on its contribution to the balance of payments and its investment and job creation record."[72] But INI also loses an enormous amount of money every year; to be precise, it lost $870 million in 1978. INI most likely suffers from the diseases common to all government enterprises: inefficiency and overstaffing. Spain as a whole is a blatant example of this, perhaps more so than most industrialized nations. The Spanish administration employs more than 600,000 "funcionarios," about 20 percent more than needed. This is a carryover from the old Franco days when people in the government had little to do but could count on a secure job. The trend is likely to continue, both because of tradition and because of rising unemployment, which will force the government—for mostly political reasons—to maintain its present levels of employment.

The year 1979 was marked by the accumulation of a heavy public sector deficit. This provides inflation with much of its fuel. The containment of public sector expenditures depends greatly on the efficacy of the government's economic program, Programa Económico del Gobierno. First unveiled in October 1979, the PEG brought on Suarez a hailstorm of protests, especially from the PCE and the CCOO, the Spanish Communist Party and its trade union, respectively. In a press conference, Marcelino Camacho Abad, secretary general of the CCOO, called the program "an open attack on workers' interests."[73] The socialist UGT joined the protest, but the government held its ground. With a new administration, Calvo Sotelo, among others, will attempt to achieve three main objectives in public sector finance:

—A clampdown on the controls on expenditures by making better budget estimates and by decreasing government sub-

---

[71] *Ibid.*

[72] "All the Spains: A Survey—Small-to-Medium is Beautiful," *The Economist*, Vol. 273, No. 7105 (November 3, 1979), p. 30.

[73] David Gardner, "Spain's largest union to oppose government's economic strategy," *Financial Times*, September 11, 1979, p. 2.

sidies for the public firms. This should decrease current expenditures and help investment expenditures.

—Increasing state participation in social security financing.

—The actuation of fiscal reform so that private sector financing can be achieved more efficiently. This should relieve the fiscal pressure by about 0.3-0.5 percent on an annual basis.[74]

For the moment attention is focused on the growing public sector deficit. The Budget anticipates a deficit of around Pta 430bn, almost the same as for this year [1980]. But on present form this is most unlikely. Since 1978 the public sector deficit has been growing at an alarming rate, having almost doubled.

Two aspects are of particular concern. First, it is not so much the size of the deficit, which at under 3 per cent in relation to GDP still remains small. Rather it is the quality of the deficit, which is being caused not by increased capital spending but by seemingly uncontrollable current expenditure items like salaries (38 percent of the Budget) and funds to the new local administration and regional authorities.

Secondly, the public sector has been absorbing more and more of the increase in money supply. From only 14 per cent in 1978 the public this year is set to account for 33 percent. Parallel with this development the accumulated public debt has been rising by leaps and bounds, through the practice of the Treasury receiving bridging loans from the Bank of Spain. Four years ago the Treasury owed the Bank of Spain Pta 55bn; by the end of this year the debt will be around Pta 800bn.

The macro projections for 1981 are that inflation will be cut from this year's 15.6 per cent to 13.5 per cent, with money supply growth kept to 1980 levels of around 18 per cent. The Government believes that new indirect taxes and the increased cost of energy supplies will add under two points to the consumer price index. On this basis it has proposed a public sector wage ceiling of 12 per cent, the difference between this and the inflation rate being accounted for by the belief that salaries should absorb the extra cost of energy.

The public sector ceiling will serve as a benchmark but the unions are likely to press for pay to keep pace with inflation rather than allow it to drop in real terms.

The determining factor will be the cash-flow position of industrial companies. This year most of the industrial workforce have preferred to seek lower pay rises and preserve jobs rather than to provoke confrontation on wage demands. The number of days lost

---

[74] *Informe Económico 1979*, p. 244.

through strikes this year has declined. One eloquent indicator of the recession is in the number of requests for temporary lay-offs. In the first nine months of this year there have been 13,447 requests with 12,170 granted; in the corresponding period in 1979 only 8,000 were granted.[75]

Governmental revenues are mostly collected from taxes and national insurance contributions, which combined make up 78 percent of the total revenues. Public consumption (including staff costs and purchase of goods and services), on the other hand, made up the lion's share of public spending (37.5 percent), followed by social security benefits with 34 percent, and gross capital formation with 15 percent. The importance of the public administrations within the public sector is reflected in their accounting for 85.8 percent of revenues.

Investing in Spain

The medium-term economic plan of the government was the latest attempt by Premier Suarez to bring the country out of its present stagnation. It will be adhered to by the new government of Premier Calvo Sotelo. Indicative rather than mandatory, the plan will try to reduce unemployment "by offering incentives to employers to hire young people, creating better opportunities for women and inducing students to stay in school an additional two years."[76] It will also try to slow down the expansion of government expenditures and increase the efficiency of state-owned industry and transport by instituting value added tax (VAT) and liberalizing foreign trade to bring Spain in line with other EEC countries.

The above-mentioned measures indicate a governmental attempt to solve Spain's ills by promoting new investments. This policy is not new. In fact, it was started by Franco, who established several "investment incentive" areas. Today, there are four types of industrial incentive areas in Spain. They differ in the types of incentives offered and in the amount of aid provided by the government, but basically they are all underdeveloped areas where the unemployment rate is high and where there is urgent need of financial relief. There are no income tax holidays, but investors are eligible for a variety of tax and tariff reductions. Cash subsidies are available to companies that "move

---

[75] Graham, "Better decision-making," p. III.

[76] "Spain," *Investing, Licensing, and Trading Conditions Abroad* (Business International Corporation, September 1979), p. 3.

plants away from overcrowded industrial areas [like Madrid, Bilbao, and Barcelona] to a section of the country with a high rate of unemployment or emigration."[77]

The free market system in Spain is generally viable, even though the government exercises more power over business operations than in most other European countries. Foreign investment is welcomed, and many examples of it can be cited, as we have already seen in the case of General Motors. Other examples of foreign investment are:

— The construction of a 4.5 billion peseta float glass plant at Aviles and of a fiberglass furnace by Cristalena Española, a subsidiary owned 74 percent by the French concern Saint-Gobain-Pont-à-Mousson.

— The planned investment by Nestlé-Switzerland of 2 billion pesetas over a two-year period. Nestlé's Spanish subsidiary is now the largest Spanish food company, with 6,000 employees.

— Matsushita Electric Industrial (Japan) has been granted permission to build a factory near Gerona, thanks to its 80 percent-owned subsidiary National Panasonic de España.[78]

"Official figures on the overall profitability of foreign investment are not readily available, but U.S. Department of Commerce figures show that US investments in manufacturing earned 6% in 1978 vs. 8% in 1977."[79] There are limitations on foreign ownership or control of enterprises deemed "vital" to the country, such as arms manufacturers, newspapers, news agencies, insurance companies, air carriers, shipping companies, public service companies in general, and the media. In addition, special permission is required for investment in mining and hydrocarbons.

Capital sources in Spain are not yet as flexible as those of a modern capital market, although they are increasing rapidly, both in number and variety.[80] There are about 500 companies listed in the stock exchange system (the most important center of which is Madrid), and most of them depend on their own funds for 50 percent of financing.

---

[77] *Ibid.*, p. 20.

[78] *Ibid.*, p. 4.

[79] *Ibid.*

[80] *Ibid.*, p. 24.

To complete this overview, it might prove useful to briefly scan Table III-18, which gives the corporate tax structure in Spain, a crucial factor for any investor in the Iberian kingdom.

TABLE III-18
Spain: Corporate Tax Rates

Corporate Tax Base	Annual worldwide income, with credit for foreign income tax paid. One-third of dividends received from affiliates more than 25 percent owned are deductible.
Corporate Tax Rate	36 percent plus 10 percent surtax on profits more than 8 percent of December 31, 1977 fiscal capital and reserves.
Major Local Income Tax Rate	Firms are subject to local tax prepayments that are credited against income tax. Prepayments are levied on different sources of income (rural and urban land, professional activities, business income, movable capital).
Income Tax on Branches	Same as for corporations.
Tax Loss Carry-forward	Five years forward; no carry-back.
Depreciation	Straight-line method only, with rate calculated according to company's location and number of shifts worked. Base annual rates: factories, 5 percent; offices, plants, and machinery, 8 percent; trucks, 20 percent; 20 percent allowance for new installation expenses. Buildings and heavy equipment benefit from an additional write-off of 2.5 percent and 6 percent, respectively.
Valuation of Inventory	At lower of cost or market value; write down from cost to market not deductible. First in First Out or other justifiable methods acceptable but not Last in Last Out.
Annual Tax on Capital	None.
Effective Withholding Taxes on Dividends under Treaty with	United States — 15 percent.
	United Kingdom — 15 percent.
	Switzerland — 15 percent; 10 percent if at least 25 percent owned by recipient.
	France — 15 percent; 10 percent if at least 25 percent owned by recipient.
	Germany — 15 percent; 10 percent if at least 25 percent owned by recipient.
	Sweden — 15 percent; 10 percent if at least 50 percent owned by recipient.
	Netherlands — 15 percent; 10 percent if at least 25 percent owned by recipient; 5.5 percent for holding companies.
	Belgium — 15 percent.
	Italy — 15 percent.
	No Treaty — 15 percent.

Source: "Spain," *Business Europe*, September 15, 1978, p. 293.

CONCLUSION

Spain has emerged from both political and economic isolation since the death of Generalissimo Franco in 1975. In a few short years it has achieved democracy and has begun to experience the good and evil of an open economy. All the problems notwithstanding, it can be said that Spain has fared well in this troubled period. It is no small achievement to have come so far so fast amid political turmoil, centrifugal regionalist forces with terroristic backlashes, and petroleum crises. Now Spain must look to the future, to an era of more regulation and to its inevitable membership in the EEC.

At present, Spain's most pressing problem is unemployment.

> Both the Government and the trade unions are equally perturbed by the employment situation. In a medium-term forecast going up to 1985, maintaining the same or slightly increased productivity rates, the Government sees the unemployment reaching 12% in the worst hypothesis and nearly 8% in the best, unless changes are made in economic policy. It is against this background of shrinking demand that the trade unions, already concerned at the effects of technological choice (particularly as regards to computerization) on employment, are calling for a reappraisal of the question of productivity, not merely as regards its material aspects, but from the over-all viewpoint of a redistribution of work ("less work for the few but more work for all") and an improvement in living and working conditions.[81]

The industrialized structure of Spain is characterized by some special features, which are noted here and commented on in terms of potential economic improvements.

— 93.4 percent of all industrial firms employ less than twenty-five people. Aside from losing the vitality and the flexibility provided to the economy by these small enterprises, it must be noted that their very existence will be jeopardized by membership in the EEC because of competition from the larger Community firms; also, they have a low level of capitalization, an inadequate level of management and marketing, problems in accession to the financial markets, and a heavy burden of welfare and social service payments. In short, they must be restructured in some way if they are to survive, and their survival is vital to Spain.

— The penetration of foreign capital is rather high. "In 1975, firms with foreign shareholdings accounted for 47% of the

---

[81] "Spain: Employment, Productivity and Industrial Relations," *Social Labour Bulletin* (ILO), No. 3 (March 1980), p. 327.

turnover of the larger Spanish firms." This is a good sign, but it must be kept in mind that the Spanish technological balance is in heavy deficit ($400 million), and this means that the Spanish economy is perhaps too highly dependent on foreign technology.

—The state has a heavy role in the economy, mostly through INI, which is responsible for one-third of all industrial investment in the country. As state enterprises are traditionally inefficient, this may present a roadblock to further development without appropriate measures.

—In addition, Spain no longer has exceptionally low wage costs; it has a productivity level lower than the EEC average; welfare and social service expenditures are very high; there seems to be no really effective financial market; and the unemployment level is soaring, especially now that emigration no longer represents an alternative to unemployment.[82]

The above structural and economic problems must be kept in mind by both Spaniards and foreign investors if these problems are to be rectified and if the general level of the economy and of life is to be brought up to EEC standards. The task may seem overwhelming, but there may also be room for cautious optimism: just as Spain emerged from thirty long years of dictatorship with a vitality that surprised many, so may it emerge from the present economic crisis with new-found energy.

---

[82] *Europe*, No. 2824 (January 11, 1980), pp. 15-16.

CHAPTER IV

Spanish Labor Law: A Review

Generalissimo Franco's death had a significant impact on the field of labor law, as well as on all other aspects of Spanish life. On April 1, 1977, a law was passed that regulates the right of association of the until then "underground" trade unions.

The 1977 law officially put an end to more than forty years of vertical trade unionism. It was followed by the passage of the all-important Workers' Statute, which went into force on March 15, 1980. These developments, together with the general turn to democracy and the promulgation of the new Spanish constitution, have brought about a changed industrial relations climate in Spain. This new climate is one of freedom of collective bargaining and has brought Spain into line with other Western European industrialized countries.

This chapter offers the reader a bird's-eye view of current Spanish labor legislation. It will also present a general picture of past labor law and its link with the present. Table IV-1 gives a chronological history of the main labor laws and orders from 1926 to the present. Included in the table are major historical and political events to provide the reader with some perspective in the matter.

TABLE IV-1

Main Labor Laws, Decrees, and Orders in Spain: 1926-Present

1902: Alfonso XIII Becomes Ruling Monarch

1926

February 19	Decree: Hygiene (Lead Compounds)
August 23	Labor Code

1927

August 15	Decree: Women (Night Work)
September 6	Decree: Women (Night Work) (Regulations)

1928

March 2	Decree: Women (Night Work)

75

TABLE IV-1 (continued)

April 1931: Abdication of King Alfonso XIII

1931

May 7	Decree: Representation of Employers and Workers (Agriculture)
May 28	Decree: Hygiene (Lead Paints)
July 1	Decree: Hours of Work (Eight-hour Day)
November 27	Act: Representation of Employers and Workers (Joint Industrial Councils)

1933

May 8	Decree: Safety (Marking of Weight)

1934

September 25	Decree: Employment of Children (Agriculture)

1936

June 18	Decree: Hours of Work (Forty-hour Week in Coal Mining)

July 1936: Breakout of Civil War

1938

March 9	Decree: Labor Charter

1939

January 5	Decree: Work Rules in Undertakings (Penalties)

April 1939: End of Civil War

September 23	Order: Apprenticeship

1940

June 7	Order: Coal Mining (Sunday Work)
October 17	Act: Labor Courts

1941

January 30	Orders: Company Stores
March 29	Decree: Wages (Fixing of Conditions of Employment)
July 11	Act: Representation of Employers and Workers (Joint Industrial Boards)
November 6	Act: Representation of Employers and Workers (Joint Industrial Boards)

1942

November 10	Act: Ministry of Labor (Province Labor Officers)

1943

February 10	Act: Employment Service

1944

January 26	Decree: Contract of Employment
March 31	Decree: Seamen's Articles of Agreement; Apprenticeship; Women and Children; Homework
July 17	Decree: Workers' Organizations (Trade Union Unity in Agriculture)

TABLE IV-1 (continued)

1945		
July 17	Charter of the Spanish People. [As amended by the Constitution of January 10, 1967]	
1947		
August 18	Decree: Works Councils	
1950		
January 9	Decree: Labor Courts (Preliminary Conciliation)	
1952		
March 28	Order: Vocational Training	
1955		
July 20	Act: Vocational Training	
1956		
October 26	Decree: Contract of Employment	
1957		
July 26	Decree: Employment of Women and Young Persons (Prohibited Types of Work)	
1958		
April 24	Act: Conciliation; Labor Courts	
May 17	Act: National Movement (Social and Labor Provisions)	
1959		
June 18	Decree No. 1036: Industrial Medicine	
1960		
May 4	Decree No. 847: Labor Council	
September 21	Decree No. 1844: Wages	
1961		
January 2	Order: Statistics Service of the Ministry of Labor	
January 12	Decree No. 20: Work Rules of Undertakings	
February 6	Order: Work Rules of Undertakings	
May 8	Order: Wages	
1962		
July 21	Act No. 39: Labor Inspection	
July 21	Act No. 41: Comanagement	
1963		
December 28	Act No. 193: Social Security (Basic Principles)	
1966		
April 21	Decree No. 907: Social Security	
May 31	Act No. 38: Social Security (Agricultural Workers)	
December 23	Decree No. 3158: Regulations under the General Social Security Scheme	
December 28	Orders: Family Assistance Benefits	

TABLE IV-1 (continued)

1967

March 2	Decree No. 443: Works Councils (Mercantile Marine)
April 20	Decree No. 779: Consolidated Texts of the Fundamental Laws

1969

May 20	Ordinance: Employment (Merchant Marine)
October 2	Order: Rural Workers
December 31	Act No. 116: Social Security (Seafarers)

1970

August 20	Decree No. 2310: Labor Rights of Working Women
December 17	Decree No. 3677: Recruitment and Employment (Fraudulent Activities) (Penalties)

1971

February 17	Act No. 2: Trade Union Act
March 9	Order: Occupational Safety and Health
March 11	Decree No. 432: Occupational Safety and Health Committees
June 9	Decree No. 1265: Trade Union Status of Alien Workers
July 21	Act No. 33: Emigration
July 23	Decree No. 1878: Trade Union Representatives (Guarantees)
July 23	Decree No. 2122: Labor Inspection (Regulations)
July 23	Decree No. 2123: Social Security (Agricultural Workers)

1972

November 2	Decree No. 3090: Employment Policy

1973

August 17	Decree No. 2380: Wages
December 19	Act No. 38: Collective Agreements

December 1972: Assassination of Carrero Blanco

1974

May 30	Decree No. 2065: Social Security
July 20	Decree No. 2487: Employment Policy
December 20	Decree No. 3526: Wage Fixing

1975

May 22	Legislative Decree No. 5: Conciliation and Arbitration
May 30	Decree No. 1148: Trade Union Rights

November 1975: Death of Francisco Franco

1976

April 8	Act No 16: Employment Relationships

TABLE IV-1 (continued)

1977	
March 4	Royal Legislative Decree No. 17: Labor-Management Relations
April 1	Act No. 19: Right of Association
April 22	Decree No. 873: Right of Association (Deposit of Rules)
June 17	Decree No. 1522: Right of Association (Civil Service)
1978	
May 2	Royal Decree No. 883: To Promote Youth Employment
July 10	Order: To Lay Down the Structure of the Social Security Authorities
September 1	Royal Decree No. 2297: To Establish an Institute for Labor Studies
October 14	Royal Decree No. 2436: To Set Up a Secretariat of State for Social Security; to Reorganize the Ministry of Health and Social Security
December 17	Constitution (Rights to Strike, and to Associate, among others)
1979	
January 26	Royal Legislative Decree No. 5: Respecting the Establishment of a Mediation, Arbitration, and Conciliation Institute
1980	
March 15	"Workers' Statute": To Regulate Collective Bargaining and Labor Relations in General

Sources: International Labour Organisation, *Legislative Series: Chronological Index of Legislation, 1919-1978* (Geneva: International Labour Office, 1980); ILO, *1979 Legislative Series* (Geneva: International Labour Office, 1980), p. 31; ILO, *1980 Legislative Series: Annual Supplement* (Geneva: International Labour Office, 1981), p. 34; "Spain: Workers' Statute," *Social and Labour Bulletin* (ILO), No. 3 (September 1980), p. 270.

PAST LABOR LEGISLATION

The end of the nineteenth and the beginning of the twentieth centuries saw the enactment of the first labor-related laws. Established in this period were laws on the hours and the conditions of work of miners (1875), compensation to workmen (1900), and maximum adult hours of working time (1919). In 1919, Spain ratified the part of the Versailles Treaty that provided for the creation of the International Labor Organization (ILO), and thus became a member of that body; while in 1920, the Ministry of Labor was created.[1]

---

[1] R. Blanpain, ed., "Spain," *International Encyclopaedia for Labour Law and Industrial Relations*, Vol. 5 (The Netherlands: Kluwer, 1977), p. 25.

The Civil War erased all past laws and practices. Unions were outlawed, and in their stead compulsory bodies or "sindicatos," comprised of both employers and employees, were set up.

The 1958 Collective Bargaining Act regulated negotiated wages, hours, and working conditions, and made a strong distinction between the so-called social and economic sections of the "sindicatos." These two sections were, in effect, respectively the trade unions and the employers' federations.[2] This was the first act of the Franco government specifically dealing with labor.

Before 1958, Spanish labor relations were guided by one of the Fundamental Acts called the Fuero del Trabajo, which was enacted on March 9, 1958, and modified by a national referendum in 1966. Fueros are primarily distinguished by the fact that they cannot be abrogated except by a national referendum. In fact, "court decisions declared very early that the provisions of the Fuero [del Trabajo, but the same became true for other Fueros] were not directly applicable by the courts, nor directly mandatory to the citizens, but that, rather, they were recommendations addressed to the legislative power of the State and that they needed implementation through normal legislative proceedings."[3]

THE CONSTITUTION

The new Spanish constitution was passed in 1978 and represents a "front of an equilibrium of forces, of a consensus, but at the same time leaves the door open to new developments. We could say that it allows, in its text, for progress of a plan for industrial democracy."[4] Several of the constitution's most important provisions apply to labor relations. They lay the groundwork for future legislation, some of which has already been enacted (e.g., the Workers' Statute). These provisions are listed in Table IV-2.

Besides those listed in Table IV-2, the constitution contains provisions against discrimination because of sex, race, religion, etc., as well as provisions that benefit Spanish workers abroad. It is a modern piece of legislation that basically replaces the

---

[2] *Ibid.*, p. 25.

[3] *Ibid.*, p. 32.

[4] Nicolas Sartorius (national secretary of the CCOO), "Industrial Democracy in Spain," mimeographed (Paper delivered at the Symposium for Industrial Democracy, organized by the Italian Communist Trade Union CGIL, Rome, May 22-23, 1980).

Fueros of pre-democracy Spain and that hopefully will set the basis for several important and far-reaching laws along the lines of the Workers' Statute.

TABLE IV-2
Selected Provisions of the Constitution

Article 7	Spells out freedom of association for the trade unions and for the employers' associations.
Article 28	Allows for the right to join a union and to strike. Also states that "no one will be forced to join a union" and that the law may limit the right to join a union for members of the armed forces and civil service employees.
Article 37	States that "the law will guarantee the rights to collective negotiations between the workers and the employers," and that measures for dealing with collective conflicts will also be permitted, subject to certain limitations yet to be established.
Article 40	Guarantees professional training and/or retraining, as well as hygiene on the job. Also provides for "necessary periods of rest" and for a framework that will promote "favorable conditions for economic and social progress."
Articles 41 to 129	Allow for social security benefits, especially in cases of unemployment.
Articles 52, 129, 131	Set up a general framework for sound economic policy and lay down the responsibilities of unions and employers' associations in such a framework.

Source: Unofficial translation of the Spanish constitution, mimeographed, obtained from Spanish embassy, in author's possession.

THE WORKERS' STATUTE

The Workers' Statute, implemented on March 15, 1980, has rendered most of the past labor-related legislation obsolete. It is an all-encompassing document in the field of labor relations. It "gives effect to the basic principles laid down by the Constitution of 1978 and to most of the clauses of the first UGT-CEOE framework agreement signed in July 1979."[5] (For a detailed description of the UGT-CEOE agreement, see Chapter V.)

The Workers' Statute applies to all workers bound by a contract of employment but excludes civil servants, senior executives,

[5] "Spain: Workers' Statute," *Social and Labour Bulletin* (ILO), No. 3 (September 1980), p. 266.

domestic staff, prisoners, performers, and professional athletes.[6] It is divided into three titles, which deal with individual contract rights, rights of assembly and of collective representation, and the regulation of collective bargaining, respectively (see Table IV-3). Basically, the Workers' Statute is Spain's equivalent of the U.S. Taft-Hartley Act, although it is very much different both in scope and in its provisions and is in many ways more comparable to Italy's Law 300 of 1970, which is also known as the "Workers' Statute."

TABLE IV-3
Selected Provisions of the Workers' Statute

Title One: The Individual Employment Relationship	
Article 1	Establishes the jurisdiction of the law, which covers private employment only.
Article 4	Lists the rights of the workers, which include "the rights to work, join a union, bargain collectively, strike and participate in the running of the firm."
Article 6	Prohibits the employment of persons under sixteen years of age. Also establishes that persons aged sixteen to eighteen can work only with parental permission, cannot work overtime, and cannot be asked to do exceptionally hard or dangerous work.
Article 27	Regulates the setting of the minimum wage by requiring that the consumer price index, the national average of labor productivity, the increment in the percentage of personal income in the gross domestic product, and the general state of the economy are to be the key criteria in minimum wage determination. These guidelines are not rigid, however; thus, the actual amount of the minimum wage will be at the discretion of the government.
Article 28	Requires equal pay for equal work.
Article 33	Establishes a "Guaranteed Wage Fund" as an autonomous organization within the Ministry of Labor. The fund provides up to four months' pay for workers who are jobless because of insolvency, bankruptcy, or suspension of salary payments. In addition, this article provides for a maximum of one year's pay to workers who have been unjustly dismissed.
Article 34	Delineates a maximum workweek of forty-three hours.
Article 35	Permits a maximum of two hours overtime per day, fifteen per month, one hundred per year, with the stipulation that the government be able to decrease

[6] *Ibid.*

TABLE IV-3 (continued)

	or even eliminate the amount of overtime in order to increase the opportunities for employing workers who have been forcibly unemployed.
Article 36	Allows management to establish flexible hours, including shiftwork, if necessary.
Article 38	Sets the minimum number of vacation days at twenty-three, including Saturdays and Sundays.
Articles 39 and 40	Deal with functional and geographical mobility, respectively. Following the practices of most other European countries, these articles make it difficult for a company to move workers from one plant to another without the concurrence of the workers and unions.
Articles 49 to 54	Deal with the termination of the contract because of technological or economic causes or because of force majeure. The law makes dismissals in general very difficult. Article 54 deals specifically with discharge for disciplinary reasons.
Article 56	Provides for pay indemnity for workers who have been discharged unjustly, as determined by the courts. Management must pay the employee the equivalent of forty-five days of salary for each year of service; however, management is not obligated to reinstate the worker.

Title Two: The Rights of Collective Representation and Workers' Assembly

Article 64	Describes the jurisdiction of the workers' council. This includes, among other duties, receiving information concerning the economic status of the firm, examining the balance sheets and other financial statements, and ensuring that labor law, social security, employment, and security provisions are enforced.
Article 65	Defines the composition of the workers' councils as follows:

    5 members in undertakings having 50 to 100 workers
    9   "   "   100 to 250
    13   "   "   251 to 500
    17   "   "   501 to 750
    21   "   "   751 to 1000

In undertakings with more than 1000 workers, 2 members per 1000 workers or fraction thereof will be elected.

Articles 67 to 76	Define the rules to be followed in the elections of the workers' councils.
Article 77	Specifically gives workers the right to meet in general assembly in "undertakings or centers of work."

TABLE IV-3 (continued)

Title Three: Regulation of Collective Bargaining

Article 85	Determines that "within the framework of the law, collective agreements may regulate economic, employment, union and welfare matters, and in general any issue relating to conditions of employment, to relations between workers and their representatives, and to managements and representative management associations."
Article 87	Deals with the legitimation issue and determines who may take part in the negotiations. Because of great debates between the political parties (see Chapter V), it was finally struck as a compromise between the wishes of the PSOE and the UCD, on the one side, and those of the PCE on the other.
Article 88	Specifies the exact composition of the negotiating committees on both the union and employer sides.
Article 89 to 92	State that all collective agreements must be registered with the Instituto de Mediación, Arbitración y Conciliación and must be published in the office gazette of the state or province to which they apply.
	The law also establishes that non-signatory parties may adhere to a collective agreement and that the "Labour Minister may extend the provisions of a collective agreement which is already in force to other undertakings and workers, with the consent of a joint committee comprising the most representative management associations and unions in the undertakings concerned."

Sources: "Spain: Workers' Statute—Part 1: Individual Relations," *European Industrial Relations Review*, No. 76 (May 1980), p. 5; "Spain's 'Workers' Statute,' Extracts from the Law of 15 March 1980," *European Industrial Relations Review*, No. 78 (July 1980), p. 26; "Spain: 'Workers' Statute,'" *Social and Labour Bulletin* (ILO), No. 3 (September 1980), p. 270.

Collective Bargaining under the Workers' Statute

Article 87 of Title Three is one of the more interesting articles of the Workers' Statute because it determines who may take part in collective bargaining. Together with Article 88, it lays down the structure of the bargaining process, some aspects of which have already been implemented in some form or another since Franco's death. Because of the importance of Articles 87 and 88, as well as the complexity of their language, both are reproduced in their entirety below.

Article 87. Legitimation

The following bodies/persons may take part in negotiations:
(1) The works council, the workers' delegates or union representatives in agreements covering an undertaking or having a more limited scope of application. In the case of agreements covering all

workers in an undertaking, the union representatives must, together, control the majority of seats on the works council. In any case, it is required that both sides acknowledge each other as negotiating parties.

(2) In order to negotiate agreements having a wider scope of application than that mentioned in paragraph (1) above, the unions, federations or confederations of unions must represent at least 10% of the members of the works council or workers' delegates. Likewise, the relevant management associations must represent at least 10% of the undertakings to which the agreement will apply.

In the case of national agreements, unions or management associations from self-governing communities must represent at least 15% of the members of the works council, the workers' delegates or management of the undertakings in the relevant sector affiliated to national federations or confederations.

(3) Any union, federation or confederation of unions and management associations which fulfills these requirements, shall have the right to take part in the negotiating committee.

Article 88. Negotiating Committee

(1) In agreements covering a single undertaking, or having a more limited scope of application, a negotiating committee shall be constituted, on the one side, by management or their representatives, and, on the other, by the representatives of workers as provided for by paragraph (1) of Article 87.

In the case of agreements having a wider scope, the negotiating committee shall be constituted when the unions, the federation or confederations of unions and management associations referred to in Article 87, represent an absolute majority among members of the works council or workers' delegates and a majority among management of the undertakings covered by the agreement.

(2) The parties to the negotiations shall appoint members to the negotiating committee. The committee shall elect a chair-person and may permit advisers to participate, without a vote, in the negotiating process.

(3) The membership of the negotiating committee shall not exceed 12, in the case of agreements covering a single undertaking, and 15, in the case of other agreements.

(4) The negotiating committee may appoint a chairperson, who may participate in the negotiations but shall not vote. If the parties decide to appoint, instead of elect, the chairperson, they shall agree on the procedure for chairing the meetings. This shall be agreed to and duly minuted in the session establishing the committee. The minutes shall be signed by representatives of both sides and by the committee's secretary.[7]

---

[7] "Spain's 'Workers' Statute,' Extracts from the Law of 15 March 1980," *European Industrial Relations Review*, No. 78 (July 1980), pp. 22-27.

Negotiation is divided into three levels, much along the lines of the Italian system. From the top down, the three types of agreements are: *national agreements,* negotiated between the employer federations and the national trade union confederations (an example of this type of agreement would be the Acuerdo Marco between the CEOE and the UGT, or the new Social Contract recently agreed upon by the UGT, the CCOO, the CEOE, and the government—both explained in the next chapter); *company-wide agreements,* such as an agreement between the Sociedad Española de Automóviles de Turismo (SEAT) and the Workers' Commissions (Comisiones Obreras—CCOO); and the *plant-by-plant agreements.*

The issues discussed in the three types of agreements obviously vary because of the differences in scope and importance of each level. The national agreements provide a standard within which company-wide agreements may be concluded. The range of issues covered include general pay increases, working hours reductions, productivity deals, disputes settlement procedures, etc., and often such issues as industrial democracy.[8]

In contrast, the company-wide agreements and the individual plant agreements deal with the specifics of a particular industry and with individual contractual rights. It must be pointed out that the company-wide agreements may sometimes be replaced in part by industry-wide compacts, such as those between the metalworkers' federation of the UGT and a united front of auto or steel manufacturers, for example.

These industry-wide agreements are very common in Italy, but most likely will have trouble gaining importance in Spain. The reason for this is that, often in Italy the three main confederations join together to present a common industrial platform. This is the case, for example, with the Metalworkers' Federation (Federazione Lavoratori Metalmeccanici—FLM), which is composed of the three individual metalworkers' federations affiliated with the three major workers' federations (i.e., the communist Confederazione Generale Italiana del Lavoro, the ex-Christian Democrat Confederazione Italiana Sindacati Lavoratori, and the socialist Unione Italiana del Lavoro). In Spain, there seems to be little chance, at least in the foreseeable future, that in each industry the various industry-wide federations of the CCOO, the UGT, and the Unión Sindical Obrera (USO) will band together.

---

[8] "Spain: Workers' Statute—Part 1: Individual Relations," *European Industrial Relations Review,* No. 76 (May 1980), p. 23.

OTHER LABOR LEGISLATION

The Workers' Statute is a very extensive piece of legislation, but there are some areas of labor law that are covered by other decrees and acts. Some of the most important are discussed below.

The Royal Legislative Decree of March 4, 1977, regulates the right to strike and sets forth disputes settlement procedure. Preventive or offensive lockouts are not authorized, except if there is danger of damage to people or property, or if occupation of the workplace is threatened.[9]

The already mentioned act of April 1, 1977, grants the freedom of association. The state Mediation, Arbitration and Conciliation Institute (Instituto de Mediación, Arbitración y Conciliación—IMAC), set up on January 26, 1979, by a decree of the Council of Ministers, is an autonomous body attached to the Ministry of Labor. IMAC must not be confused with the separate Interconfederal Committee on Mediation, Arbitration, and Conciliation, which was set up in January 1980 jointly by the UGT and the CEOE to interpret the provisions of the Acuerdo Marco and of subsequent agreements that may be signed.[10]

There has been considerable disagreement over the procedural rules of IMAC; therefore, the institute has been unable to perform its main function: that of resolving collective disputes. Most of its work is concerned instead with attempting to resolve individual disputes.[11]

IMAC is required to:

1. Not interfere with the free exercise of labor rights.
2. Act only upon specific requests from workers or management or their representative bodies. (In special cases, IMAC may act on its own initiative, thus allowing for some kind of compulsory arbitration.)
3. Always be impartial and professional.[12]

---

[9] "New Decree to Regulate Labour Relations," *Social and Labour Bulletin* (ILO), No. 2 (June 1977), pp. 124-126.

[10] "Establishment of a New Joint Mediation, Conciliation and Arbitration Body," *Social and Labour Bulletin* (ILO), No. 2 (June 1980), p. 169.

[11] "Spain Disputes Resolution," *European Industrial Relations Review*, No. 85 (February 1981), p. 13.

[12] *Ibid.*, p. 14.

Special labor tribunals for arbitration have also been set up by the IMAC decree-law wherever there is a labor court. Decisions from these labor tribunals are legally binding.

> Workers and management may bring either individual or collective disputes to these tribunals so long as an attempt is first made to resolve disputes via an IMAC official. This latter procedure is now termed "conciliation" and refers to the attempt to resolve a dispute via discussions with a third party, with the intention of resorting to arbitration if necessary.[13]

IMAC is also required to mediate collective disputes and serve as a central depository for statutes of trade unions, statutes of employers' organizations, collective agreements, and official documents of electoral results of workers' councils data.[14]

The Spanish equivalent of the Occupational Safety and Health Act is the Ordenanza General de Seguridad e Higiene en el Trabajo (OSH), which was approved during the Franco era by the Ministry of Labor on March 9, 1971, and is still extant today.[15] Finally, there is no equivalent of the Landrum-Griffin Act, as can well be understood, since the powerful unions would strongly and forcefully object to the passing of any law that would impose rules on their internal structure.

THE COURTS AND THE LABOR MINISTRY

"The Spanish system of law is not based upon any 'share decision' or judicial precedent rule. Court decisions solve the case in hand, and they are not a rule for further cases with different parties."[16] This means that the courts are to apply only a preestablished written code, at least in theory. In practice, there is a system of judicial precedent, since the Supreme Court does make decisions that are followed by lower courts in judging similar cases.

The general principles of Spanish labor law refer back to the civil code. The system of Spanish labor law is, however, presently built on a solid framework of labor-specific laws.

Disputes that arise in the field of labor are settled by a "highly developed and popular system of Labour Courts."[17] There are

---

[13] *Ibid.*
[14] *Ibid.*
[15] Blanpain, ed., *International Encyclopaedia*, Vol. 5, p. 7.
[16] *Ibid.*, p. 38.
[17] *Ibid.*, p. 98.

three levels of labor courts; from the lowest to the highest they are as follows:

—the Magistratura de Trabajo (Labor Court)
—the Tribunal Central de Trabajo (Central Labor Court)
—Sala de lo Social del Tribunal Supremo (Social Chamber of the Supreme Court)

There is at least one labor court in each of the fifty Spanish provinces. The Central Labor Court is comprised of thirty-one judges, each with at least ten years' experience in a labor court. It is made up of four chambers, which deal with dismissal cases, labor cases excluding those dealing with dismissals, and social security cases. The Social Chamber of the Supreme Court has eleven judges, three of which must have previously been labor judges.

The number of cases handled by these three types of courts is enormous. The Magistraturas de Trabajo handle an average 200,000 cases a year; the Tribunal Central, about 6,000 cases; and the Sala de lo Social adjudicates over 500 to 600 cases a year.[18]

The two higher courts are appellate courts, but no appeal can be made from the Tribunal Central to the Supreme Court as such. Appeals can be made from the lower courts to the higher courts, but only in accordance with certain regulations. The attorney general of Spain is "empowered to present a very peculiar type of appeal, the 'appeal in the interest of the law' (recurso en interés de la ley), if he thinks that legal rules established in a Central Labor Court decision are erroneous." [19]

The Labor Ministry must inspect factories or workplaces to ascertain if they are in compliance with the law. The Labor Ministry also has the power to sanction any violation of the law and to interpret "by Way of a General Interpretation of Labour Rules." [20] In addition, the Labor Ministry has either jurisdiction over or connection with the Spanish Institute of Immigration (Instituto Español de Emigración), the Institute for Labor Studies (Instituto de Estudios Laborales), and the National Fund for the Protection of Work (Fondo Nacional de Protección al Trabajo).

---

[18] *Ibid.*, pp. 102-104.

[19] *Ibid.*, p. 103.

[20] *Ibid.*, p. 28.

CONCLUSION

It is short of miraculous that Spain was able to undergo the transition from highly regulated, vertically structured, and government-controlled labor laws and unions to a modern, rather chaotic, and very complex labor relations system. Five short years were enough to see many trade unions firmly established and fighting among each other because of different political and economic ideologies. These trade unions, especially the UGT and the CCOO, exerted a great deal of influence in both the passage of the constitution and of the Workers' Statute, thus molding the shape of future labor disputes and settlements. The UGT perhaps went one step further and guided specific aspects of labor legislation by concluding, to date, two Acuerdo Marcos with the CEOE.

These accomplishments should be viewed as very important and very constructive for the continuing development of Spanish democracy. They must, however, not be perceived as developments that have solved the problems of Spanish labor relations, which heretofore had been immersed in the Dark Ages. On the contrary, the new labor legislation must be taken as a starting point from and by which new problems can be solved.

In addition, the changeover from pre- to post-Franco laws and labor relations did not happen overnight. It was in the making for a long time, and the Spanish unions now so alive and well had for many years been preparing themselves in exile for a grand reentry. Unions, government, and employers' confederations must now face up to the enormous problems of inflation, unemployment, and terrorism that are crippling the country. Only through diligent application of present legislation and intelligent cooperation will they be able to achieve successful solutions.

CHAPTER V

Organized Labor in Spain

The trade union movement in Spain is, and has been, not only very powerful, but also rich in tradition and integral to Spanish life. The major labor federations took an active part in the Civil War; thus, it was mainly against them that the suppression of the Franco dictatorship was directed. Starting in 1936 and lasting for more than thirty years thereafter, the trade union movement was forced to go underground. Threatened with prison terms or possibly death, its main leaders had to operate either from abroad or clandestinely. As proof of the vitality of the labor movement, however, there was a resurgence of trade unionism on a large scale as soon as Spain returned to democracy.

Although now very much changed and operating along the lines of labor movements in other industrialized nations, Spanish labor unions are taking an active part in molding Spain's future. With close political ties, the various trade union confederations had much to say about the drafting of the recently approved Workers' Statute, and undoubtedly were very influential in drafting some articles of the Spanish constitution.

To allow for a smooth transition from dictatorship to democracy, as well as to prove their high degree of social consciousness, Spanish labor refrained from major strike activity up until the end of 1977, even though such a stipulation was not officially included in the Moncloa Pact. Parenthetically, it must also be said that Spanish labor was neither sufficiently strong nor enough organized to successfully initiate effective strikes during that period, but this notwithstanding, it did try to restrain workers' protests.

This chapter describes Spain's major labor federations, including their history and their affiliations to international trade union movements. An attempt will be made to clarify the impact and influence of these labor federations on the history and future of Spain. The latter will be of special interest, since the importance of the labor movement in Spain and its role in Spanish society has been somewhat unique.

HISTORICAL OVERVIEW

Agrarian uprisings in Andalusia and the formation of a Barcelona textile workers' association were the first visible signs of the infant Spanish labor movement, as early as 1840. In 1868, two anarchistic labor organizations were formed: The International Working Men's Association and the secret Socialist Democratic Alliance (Alianza de la Democracia Socialista). The former was outlawed in 1872, but the latter survived until 1888, with a claimed peak membership of 300,000.[1]

The history of modern Spanish trade unionism begins the same year, precisely on August 12, 1888, when delegates representing 44 different associations with 4,668 affiliated members convened at the Socialist Club of Barcelona, in Catalonia, to open the first National Workers' Congress. It was there that Pablo Iglesias, a major labor leader, suggested the name General Spanish Workers' Union (Unión General de Trabajadores de España—UGT) for the first labor confederation. The name was accepted and, as is well known, has persisted until the present day.

In contrast to the founders of the UGT, the anarchistic leaders of Spain, in keeping with their ideals, proclaimed that there was no need for a centralized labor federation. In 1911, however, perhaps motivated by the success of the UGT, which had become their main rival, the anarchists decided to form the National Confederation of Labor (Confederación Nacional del Trabajo— CNT). The CNT was also founded in Catalonia, and it was influenced by the French General Workers' Confederation (Confédération Générale du Travail—CGT), which at that time defined itself as a syndicalist-revolutionary trade union.[2]

The CNT played a major role in the great series of strikes of 1917 that began to split the Spanish people into leftist and rightist factions. Led by the Iberian Anarchist Federation (Federación Anarquista Iberica—FAI), a political group, the CNT attempted, through strikes and sporadic violence, to set up a communist

---

[1] A. P. Coldrick and Philip Jones, eds., *International Directory of the Trade Union Movement* (New York: Facts on File, 1979), p. 973.

[2] Guy Desotre, *Les Organisations Syndicales des Pays Candidats á l'Adhesion anx Communantes Europeenes: Les Syndicats en Espagne* (Brussells: Institut d' Etudes Europeennes, 1978), p. 2.

anarchistic regime in several Spanish regions, especially Catalonia and Andalusia. These attempts met with some success because of the appeal of the anarchistic ideals to many regional groups. As has already been discussed, there existed, and still exists, many groups in Spain with strong nationalist and self-governing ideals, groups that live in isolation from the central government, often in collectivistic communal setups in small villages.

By the eve of the Civil War, the CNT was beginning to lose ground to the UGT, which was better organized and which tried to promote political reform without resorting to violence. The UGT had acquired strength through the creation of the Casas del Pueblo (People's Houses), which were centers for cultural and recreational gatherings, and also through participation in the great metalworkers' strikes in Bilbao. It had more than 200,000 members in 1918, and almost one-half million before the start of the Civil War.[3]

Although this will take us out of the historical narrative, the problem of the Casas del Pueblo should be noted here. They were expropriated by the Franco dictatorship at the end of the Civil War, and today present a difficult and apparently unsolvable problem. The UGT claims that the property and the finances of the Casas del Pueblo belong to it as the "historical heir" of the pre-Civil War UGT. The Workers' Commissions (Comisiones Obreras—CCOO) argue, however, that the Casas del Pueblo belong to the Spanish labor movement in general and thus should be split among all labor confederations now extant. It can well be imagined what controversies such a problem can stir up. This is especially true because Spanish unions are relatively poor and often rely more on contributions than on dues to replenish their treasuries; the patrimony of the Casas has been estimated at between 6,240 and 8,000 million pesetas.[4] The ownership of the Casas del Pueblo and of all their assets would give the UGT an enviable financial position that could easily be exploited to the detriment of the CCOO in the fight for trade union hegemony.

The third oldest trade union in Spain is the Solidarity of Basque Workers (Euska Langilla Alkartasuna-Solidaridad de Trabajadores Vascos—ELA/STV), also founded in 1911 and primarily concerned with the welfare of the workers in the Basque region. It is a relatively moderate union with a left-of-center ideology and

---

[3] *Ibid.*, p. 3.

[4] "Franco lo incautó y Suarez no lo devuelve," *UGT Bulletin*, No. 407 (April 1979), pp. 4-6.

strongly attached to the National Basque Party (Partido Nacionalista Vasco—PNV), which often aligns itself with the Union of the Democratic Center (Unión de Centro Democratico—UCD), at least on national issues.

The Civil War saw the birth of many civilian militias, which divided themselves along anarchistic, socialist, and communist lines. Workers from the UGT and the CNT flocked to their respective military organizations, ready to defend the republic. This attachment to separate political ideologies, however, caused a great deal of confusion, and the Republican Army was basically split into three disorganized factions. Only the Communists, with the help of Moscow advisers, managed some semblance of cohesion, especially in the latter years of the war. It was from that moment onward that the communist movement started to gain ground in Spain, mainly to the detriment of the CNT.

When the Civil War finally ended, Franco lost no time and, with a decree issued on September 13, 1936, outlawed the CNT, the UGT, and the ELA/STV. In 1939 he implemented a law to confirm the 1936 decree, and another to confiscate all trade union property, including the UGT's Casas del Pueblo. Every asset was transferred to the Falange, the monolithic party that ruled Spain until Franco's death. A "vertical trade union" was subsequently set up, in 1940, and given the name Spanish Syndical Organization (Organización Sindical Española—OSE).[5] Until 1977, the OSE was the only legal bargaining agent between labor and management. Actually, it was not at all a real "bargaining agent" in today's sense of the word. All employers and employees were obliged to belong to the OSE, and all officers of the trade unions were appointed by the government. The supreme authority of the OSE was delegated to the National Trade Union Delegation (Delegación Nacional de Sindicatos—DNS), in which both the so-called economic (in reality management) and social (i.e., labor) sectors were represented.

The DNS was managed by a secretary general and was divided into four sectors: social, economic, administrative, and syndical. The national "sindicatos," or vertical industry-wide organizations, were similarly organized and at each level were advised by joint boards representing both labor and management. From these boards were chosen the 150 representatives of the OSE to the Cortes of the Franco era, then only a rubber-stamp parliament.[6]

---

[5] Also known as the Confederación Nacional de los Sindicatos (CNS).

[6] Eugene K. Keefe et al., *Area Handbook for Spain* (Washington, D.C.: U.S. Government Printing Office, 1976), p. 249.

Such a system was more a method of controlling labor than a way for real trade unionism to become established. During this period, the UGT, CNT, and ELA/STV leaders refused any cooperation with the OSE and went into exile. Several were imprisoned or killed. The Communists, on the other hand, tried to influence the OSE by illegally and loosely organizing the workers. The Communists long labored underground and finally acquired importance during the strikes of 1961 and 1962, the first large-scale work stoppages of the Franco era.

The strikes were guided by committees elected in the assemblies of protesting workers. These committees provided the shopfloor workers with an alternative to official trade unions. By 1964, almost all these committees, which were formed during strikes and periods of calm, were under Communist control. They organized themselves into what has now become known as the CCOO.

During the unrest at the end of the Franco regime, the so-called forces of the "Catholic left" also tried to establish themselves in the workplace. In 1961, young Christian workers and some UGT splinter groups formed the Syndical Workers' Union (Unión Sindical Obrera—USO), which defined itself as anticapitalist, aconfessional, and socialist. USO militants participated in the social unrest described in the preceding paragraph. They became members of the strikers' committees up until 1965, when they decided to abandon them because of excessive communist influence.[7]

At present, the USO is trying to appeal to the same workers who are drawn by the UGT, and thus there exists a strong antagonism between the two unions. It is interesting to note that, in 1978, Suarez's government tried—unsuccessfully it seems—to pick up the USO's banner at a time when the UCD was trying to form a union of its own, in order to emulate the Partido Comunista Español (PCE) ties with the CCOO and the Partido Socialista Obrero Español (PSOE) ties with the UGT. Today, the USO remains officially unaffiliated to any political party, unlike any other major trade union federation. It has been reported, however, that it has some indirect ties with the UCD, especially since receiving help from the ruling party prior to the 1980 trade union elections.

---

[7] George Couffignal, "Il Sindacato in Spagna dopo la Morte di Franco," *Quaderni Sindacali*, No. 80 (September-October 1979), p. 168.

SPANISH UNIONS TODAY

After the death of Franco, a proliferation of labor organizations emerged in Spain. To the old established ones such as the UGT, the ELA/STV, the CNT, and the Catalonian Workers' Solidarity (Solidaridad d'Obrera de Catalunya—SOC)—which had been founded in 1956, primarily to safeguard the welfare of the Christian Catalonian workers—and to the relatively newer ones, such as the CCOO and the USO, were added small extremist confederations such as the Confederation of Unitary Unions of Workers (Confederación de Sindicatos Unitarios de Trabajadores—CSUT), the Unitary Unions (Sindicatos Unitarios—SU), and several of what are called "sindicatos amarillos" (yellow trade unions), which are, in fact, company unions. (For a detailed profile of the Spanish unions, see Tables V-1 to V-3.)

TABLE V-1
Major Labor Confederations in Spain

Name	Workers' Commissions (Comisiones Obreras—CCOO)
Address	Batalla del Salado, 42 Madrid 7 Tel: 407-5360/5472 (secretary general, organization, education) 408-4382/4502 (international relations, information and press)
Estimated Membership	1.5 to 2 million
Local Affiliations	About 20 affiliated "sindicatos." Some of the most important are: Federación Siderometalurgica (metalworkers-autoworkers) Textil Piel (textile workers) Químicas (chemical workers) Industrias Energeticas, Minerías y de la Tierra (energy, mine, and cave workers)
International Affiliations	So far none. Contacts have been maintained, however, with the World Federation of Trade Unions (WFTU) (observer status). Applied for membership to the ETUC in 1977, was refused, and has reapplied.
Leadership	Marcelino Camacho Abad, secretary general, ex-PCE deputy (Madrid); Nicolas Sartorius, policy secretary; Serafin Aliaga, international secretary
General Observations	Communist-dominated, very close ties with the PCE. So far the largest trade union confederation in Spain. Comparable to the Italian Confederazione Generale Italiana del Lavoro (CGIL).

Organized Labor in Spain

TABLE V-1 (continued)

Name	General Workers' Union (Unión General de Trabajadores de España—UGT)
Address	Joaquín García Morato, 90 Madrid, 3 Tel: 445-2566/2614/2654 (international organization) 445-6312/6373/6564 (secretary general)
Estimated Membership	1.5 to 2 million
Local Affiliations	About 16 affiliated sindicatos; most are affiliated to the respective international trade secretariats (ITSs). The most important ones are: Sindicato Minero (mine workers) Federación Nacional Sidero-Metalúrgica (metalworkers) Federación del Textil, Confección, Cuero y Calzado (textile, shoe, and leather workers) Federación de la Química (chemical workers)
International Affiliations	International Confederation of Free Trade Unions (ICFTU); ETUC; the sixteen ITSs
Leadership	Nicholas Redondo Urbieta, secretary general, PSOE deputy from Vizcaya (one of the Basque provinces); Manuel Simon Velasco, international secretary
General Observations	Socialist; one of the "historical heirs" of the Spanish trade union movement (the other is the CNT); tied to the PSOE.
Name	Workers' Syndical Union (Unión Sindical Obrera—USO)
Address	Avda. de José Antonio, 22 dup. 3 Iz. Madrid, 14 Tel.: 404-554/5612/5628
Estimated Membership	200,000
Local Affiliations	16 affiliated federaciones. The main ones are: Federación del Metal (metalworkers) Federación de Energia (energy workers)
International Affiliations	Affiliated to the following three ITSs: International Metalworkers' Federation (IMF), International Union of Food and Allied Workers' Associations (IUF), and International Federation of Chemical, Energy and General Workers' Unions (ICEF). Applied to the International Transport Workers' Federation (ITF) but, because of opposition from the UGT, was refused membership. Also applied to

TABLE V-1 (continued)

	the ETUC and the ICFTU, but was also refused membership because of UGT opposition.
Leadership	Manuel Zaguirre, secretary general; Angel Otero, international relations secretary
General Observations	Socialist and pluralist, independent from political parties. M. Zaguirre replaced J. Zufiaur, who wanted the USO to join with the UGT, in October 1977.
Name	National Confederation of Labor (Confederación Nacional de Trabajo—CNT)
Address	Princesa 56, Barcelona Calle Libertad 15, Madrid Tel.: 319-56-82
Estimated Membership	Less than 100,000
International Affiliations	Association Internationale des Travailleurs (AIT), now a quasi-extinct organization.
Leadership	Enrique Marcos, secretary general; Juan Gomez Casas, former secretary general
General Observations	Quasi-extinct organization; one of the "historical heirs" of the Spanish trade union movement; not tied to any political party; anticommunist, anticapitalist.
Name	Confederation of Unitary Unions of Workers (Confederación de Sindicatos Unitarios de Trabajadores—CSUT)
Address	Hortaleza 15, Madrid Tel.: 231-9812
Estimated Membership	Less than 100,000
International Affiliations	None
Leadership	Jeronimo Lorente, secretary general; Antonio Castillo Gerena, assistant secretary general
General Observations	"Maoist"; unitary; affiliated with the small, radical left-wing Partido de Trabajadores Español (PTE).
Name	Unitary Unions (Sindicatos Unitarios—SU)
Address	Gil de Santibanez, 4 Madrid Tel.: 226-7105
Estimated Membership	Less than 50,000

International Affiliations	None
Leadership	José Miguel Ibarrola San Martin, secretary general; Pedro Cristabal, relations secretary
General Observations	Maoist; unitary; affiliated with the radical, left-wing Revolutionary Workers' Organization and the PTE.
Sources:	Cayuela Miró, Spanish Labor Attaché to the United States, to the author, 1979; A. P. Coldrick and Philip Jones, eds., *International Directory of the Trade Union Movement* (New York: Facts on File, 1979); direct communication with confederations listed.

TABLE V-2
Regional Labor Unions

Name	Catalonian Workers' Solidarity (Solidaridad d'Obrera de Catalunya—SOC)
Address	Ausies March 35 Barcelona 10 Tel.: 226-4200/3604
Estimated Membership	Less than 10,000
International Affiliations	World Confederation of Labour (WCL); ETUC
Leadership	Josep Alameda, secretary general
General Observations	Socialist ideology, mostly concerned with the welfare of the Catalonian workers
Name	Solidarity of Basque Workers (Euska Langilla Alkartasuna-Solidaridad de Trabajadores Vascos —ELA/STV)
Address	Calle Euskaladuna Alberto Akocer 32 Apdo. 1391 Madrid 16 Bilboa, 8 (Madrid office) Vizcaya Tel.: 458-7430 Tel.: 444-2504 444-2554
Estimated Membership	100,000
Local Affiliations	10 main national "sindicatos," all of which belong to the respective ITS. The most important one is that of the metalworkers, which belongs to both the IMF and the European Metalworkers' Federation (EMF).
International Affiliations	ICFTU; WCL; ETUC-EMF; ITSs
Leadership	Manuel Robles Arangiz, president; Alfonso Echeverria, secretary general

TABLE V-2 (continued)

General Observations	Basque regional union; some ties with the moderate Basque PNV. It is interesting to note that the ELA/STV is the only union confederation in the world that is a member of both the WCL and the ICFTU.
Name	National Galician Intersyndical Union (Intersindical Nacional Galegia—ING)
General Observations	No information available except that its name appears when labor relations of Galicia are mentioned. Recently it was reported that the ING won 22.7 percent of the votes cast in Galicia for the elections of the works council representatives (1980 elections). These results were gathered when about one-half of the votes cast were counted, and placed the ING between the CCOO (28.7 percent) and the UGT (21.25 percent) in Galicia.
Sources:	Cayuela Miró, Spanish Labor Attaché to the United States, to the author; A. P. Coldrick and Philip Jones, eds., *International Directory of the Trade Union Movement* (New York: Facts on File, 1979); direct communication with some of the confederations listed.

TABLE V-3
Other "Independent" Trade Unions ("sindicatos amarillos")

Name	Democratic Confederation of Workers (Confederación Democrática de Trabajadores—CDT)
Leadership	José Manuel Alonso Fueyo, secretary-general
Name	General Confederation of Workers (Confederación General de Trabajadores—CGT)
Address	Calle Blasco de Garcy 86 Bajo, Madrid 15 Tel.: 233-9876
Leadership	Lucas Ramos García; Angel Lopez
General Observations	Non-Marxist; "independent" center-oriented union
Name	Communitary Labor Confederation (Confederación de Trabajo Commitario—CTC)
Address	Infanta Mercedes 58, 2° Izgda, Madrid Tel.: 279-3885
Leadership	Juan José Tomas Marco, secretary general
General Observations	Catholic-oriented; espouses "Christian Humanism"; non-Marxist; "independent" center-oriented union.

Organized Labor in Spain

TABLE V-3 (continued)

Name	Confederation of Independent Workers (Confederación de Trabajores Independientes—CTI)
Address	Hartzenbusch 17, 1 dcha, Madrid 10 Tel.: 445-1744
Leadership	Cerefino Maesta, secretary general
General Observations	Non-Marxist; "independent" center-oriented union
Name	Spanish Confederation of Independent Unions (Confederación Española de Sindicatos Independientos—ESI)
Address	General Pardiñas 34, Madrid 1 Tel.: 275-3250/3320
Leadership	Angel Bastante Abradelo, president; Eduardo Ramón Pimental, secretary general
General Observations	Non-Marxist; "independent" center-oriented union
Name	Federación de Trabajores de la Enseñanza del Estado Español
Address	c/o Alonso Cano 63-10 10 Madrid-3
International Affiliations	World Confederation of Teaching Professionals (WCOTP)
Name	Junta Central del Relegios de Agentes Commerciales de España
Address	Goya 55 Madrid
International Affiliations	ICCTA

Sources: Cayuela Miró, Spanish Labor Attaché to the United States, to the author, 1979; A. P. Coldrick and Philip Jones, eds., *International Directory of the Trade Union Movement* (New York: Facts on File, 1979); direct communication with some of the confederations listed.

[a] In addition to the above, there exists the Confederación General de los Cuadros, which is a managerial personnel confederation. Founded February 10, 1979, it has ties to the Confédération Internationale des Cadres, but no outright affiliation.

1978 Trade Union Elections

Between the 1977 elections of the new Cortes and the April 1979 municipal elections came the first free balloting since the Franco era for the election of union representatives to workers' councils. As can be seen in Table V-4, the CCOO carried the most votes, with the UGT ranking second by a rather wide margin. Several splinter groups and a large portion of undecided or indifferent workers completed the picture. Now the situation has changed considerably, as will be discussed later in the chapter.

TABLE V-4
Results of the 1978 Trade Union Elections [a]

Union	Number of Delegates	Percent of Vote
CCOO	47,111	37.8
UGT	38,671	31.0
Unaffiliated	15,844	12.7
USO	7,381	5.9
CSUT	5,985	4.0
SU	3,376	2.7
ELA/STV	3,140	2.5
Patriotic Workers' Commission (LAB)	771	—
CNT	339	—
Dissidents of ELA/STV (STVa)	309	—
CCT	240	—
SOG	81	—
ING	28	—
SOC	15	—

Sources: Benjamin Martin, *Labor and Politics in Spain Today* (manuscript obtained from the author); *El País*, March 28, 1978.

[a] The remaining 2,289 delegates are distributed among various organizations: independent unions and unions of specific trades or enterprises, especially those in banks, hospitals, commerce, and transport.

(—) indicates negligible amount.

It is interesting to note that the Communists, who had received a blow in the political arena by gathering only about 10 percent of the votes for their PCE, received the most votes for their trade union, the CCOO. The Communists thereby hoped to become influential in Spanish politics, if not directly, then at least indirectly.

Political Maneuvering. As it turned out, the PCE and the CCOO were not able to take full advantage of this newly-found strength because of the complex situation in the political arena. They were also hampered by the heavy influence of Suarez's government and the UCD in all aspects of Spanish life.

Premier Suarez at first sided with the PCE in the Parliament to check the advance of the PSOE and the increase in popularity of its leader, Felipe Gonzalez. Once assured of a position of strength, however, Suarez promptly switched allegiance by supporting the industrial relations pact signed between the Confederación Española de Organizaciones Empresariales (CEOE) and the UGT at the end of 1979. This political maneuvering by Suarez was done because the UCD at first needed to weaken its main political rival, the PSOE, in order to gain control of the Cortes. The switch then came because the UCD, a middle-of-the-road conservative party lacking a trade union of its own,[8] needed to side with the least extreme of the two main trade unions. Thus, an alliance with the PCE in time of need seemed an acceptable political move, but the support of a militant CCOO would have been unacceptable to the UCD base.

The political maneuvering by the UCD and by other political parties has long been a source of drawn-out disputes and discussion in the Cortes. This did not prevent the Spanish Parliament from acting on several important labor-related matters, however, as evidenced by the passage of the constitution and the Workers' Statute.

The Workers' Statute

The Workers' Statute was an important piece of legislation, over which the UGT and the CCOO battled furiously. They did so both directly and in the Cortes, by way of the PSOE and the PCE, respectively.

Prior Developments. Before the clash over this particular piece of legislation can be analyzed, however, several events must be noted. In 1977, just after the victory of the PSOE over the PCE for hegemony among leftist votes, part of the nonaligned USO joined the UGT. This defection strengthened the UGT considerably, especially from a psychological point of view. José M.

---

[8] In this context, it is interesting to note the difference in the labor-political arena of Italy and Spain. The two countries may at first sight appear very similar, but in fact are not. In Italy the three largest labor confederations have close ties with the three largest political parties. The CGIL, the CISL, and the UIL are affiliated with the PCI, the DC, and the PSI, respectively. The Socialists are the smallest of the three, both in the Parliament and in the labor field. The Communists and the Christian Democrats are of comparable size, both in Parliament, where the DC has the edge, and in industrial relations, where the CGIL has the advantage. In Spain, on the other hand, there are only two major labor confederations, the largest of which corresponds to the smallest of the three main political parties. The most important political party, the UCD, has no labor union of its own and thus lacks a great deal of leverage in the labor field.

Zufiaur, secretary general of the USO, became the UGT's number-two man when he led the group of dissenters into the UGT fold. The USO militants who joined the UGT were well organized and provided their new union with some badly needed intermediary organization.

The battle on the labor front was averted for a couple of years after the death of Generalissimo Franco primarily for two reasons. First, the democratization of Spain was implemented with a great deal of sorely needed caution by King Juan Carlos and his then prime minister, Adolfo Suarez. Both leaders managed to tread the thin line separating chaos from order in Spain. This was not an easy task given the reactionary nationalist right-wing elements and the impatient left-wing groups ready to jump at any chance to assert their strength.

Second, all political parties, once the initial situation was stabilized and a new Cortes elected, agreed to try to limit inflation by setting a ceiling on all wage increases (of 22 percent). The trade unions tacitly agreed to this, as already noted. This agreement came to be known as the Moncloa Pact, since it was arranged in the Moncloa Palace, the residence of the Spanish prime minister.

The Moncloa Pact kept the labor relations scene relatively quiet until the end of 1978, when two new controversies surfaced over which groups should have collective bargaining power—the "secciones sindicales" (trade union sections) or the mostly CCOO-controlled workers' councils—and over what issues should be discussed between the trade unions and the employers' federations. The latter was particularly important because any agreement reached between the unions and the employers would serve as a basis for almost all collective bargaining contracts.

The UGT and the CCOO were the two main opponents in this conflict. More than just a struggle over any particular subject, the clash between the UGT and the CCOO became an arm wrestling contest for trade union supremacy. All other trade unions were left far behind primarily because of the size of the CCOO and the UGT, but also because they were, and still are, the only two unions that could count on the direct support of the politically influential PCE and PSOE.

Signs of the struggle between the UGT and the CCOO had become apparent long before the above issues emerged. A controversy had arisen between the two over the method of selecting the trade union delegates to the workers' councils (see Table V-4). The PSOE and its trade union ally, the UGT, accused the government of openly discriminating in favor of the communist-controlled CCOO for having decided that the elections were to be conducted using "listas abiertas" (open lists), whereby candidates appear on the ballots solely as individuals without any reference to their organizational affiliation. The system of "listas cerradas" (closed lists), advocated by the UGT, required the organizational identity of all candidates to appear on the ballots. The communist leadership of the CCOO favored the open-list method because it permitted many of its supporters to conceal their trade union and political identities. This was a matter of some importance because many workers, when presented with a choice between a procommunist or a prosocialist candidate, would tend to vote for the noncommunist. Furthermore, the open-list method was more in line with "assemblearismo," the concept of labor unity postulated by the CCOO leadership.[9]

Debate in the Cortes. The real clash came, however, with the debate in the Cortes over the passage of the Workers' Statute. The key policy dispute was over Article 87, which deals with who has the power to negotiate labor contracts—the trade union sections or the workers' councils—both of which are established workers' representative bodies in the Spanish labor system.

The government, led by Premier Suarez, decided on this issue to abandon its policy of tacit alliance with the PCE and to back the Socialists of Felipe Gonzalez. Thus, the UCD backed the PSOE proposal that the trade union sections be the contracting agents in the collective bargaining process. The PCE, on the other hand, wanted the workers' councils, over which the CCOO has a very strong influence because of the historical development of the workers' councils, to do the bargaining.

The debate in Parliament was long and bitter. Each side claimed that democracy would be served best if its proposal was enacted. Neither side carried the day completely, and a complicated compromise was finally reached. The trade union representatives are now entitled to negotiate at a provincial, regional, or county level if they constitute at least 10 percent of the workers' councils or personnel delegates at that level. The workers' councils can, however, negotiate at a company or lower level, unless within the workers' councils there is a majority of union members. (This topic is treated more at length in Chapter IV.)

---

[9] Benjamin Martin, "Labor and Politics in Spain Today" (manuscript obtained from the author).

This compromise gives more importance to the trade union sections and thus leans toward the original government proposal. In almost all large enterprises, in fact, the workers' councils most likely will be comprised by a majority of trade union members. In addition, at almost all levels, the trade union sections will constitute at least 10 percent of the workers' councils.

It must be pointed out, however, that Spain is a country of small firms, 69.3 percent of which employ less than 250 workers.[10] In many of these firms, it is very likely that the workers' councils are not made up of a majority of trade union members, and thus that the CCOO will be able to exert a very strong influence.

The Acuerdo Marco

While the debate over Article 87 of the Workers' Statute was going on, the UGT signed an agreement with the largest and most influential of the employers' federations, the CEOE. The Acuerdo Marco, or "standard agreement," as this UGT-CEOE compact is called, sets a limit to wage hikes of 13-16 percent; proposes to lower, over a two-year period, the number of hours worked yearly from 2,000 to 1,880; proposes to minimize the amount of overtime; and sets as a goal the achievement through legislation of a lower retirement age. The last two measures were presumably agreed upon to try to decrease unemployment.[11]

These were the general, if somewhat rhetorical, lines of agreement. More important than the content of the agreement was the fact that the UGT and the CEOE agreed that collective bargaining would be negotiated between the trade union sections and management, as long as the trade unions or the managerial associations contained at least 10 percent union members.

The Acuerdo Marco is along the lines of the Workers' Statute (approved later) but tends to emphasize the trade union sections. The CCOO refused to take part in this agreement and did not sign it. It claimed that the trade union sections would be too powerful and that the workers should ask for pay hikes more on the order of 18-20 percent. Both demands were in line with the more militant stand of the CCOO and with the proposal backed by the

---

[10] José M. Arigjar, "Revolución en la Estrutura Laboral," *Historia 16*, Vol. III, No. 21 (January 1978), p. 18.

[11] "Periodico Mural de la Comisión Ejecutiva Confederal," *UGT Informa*, No. 5 (January 1980), p. 4.

PCE during the representation debate over Article 87 of the Workers' Statute.

In accordance with the Acuerdo Marco, the workers' councils would more or less be confined to consultation with management over:

—the general evolution of the economic sector pertinent to the particular firm,

—any restructuring plans, reductions of the workweek, or partial or total lockouts,

—any judicial changes of the status of the firm, and

—any proposed sanction or disciplinary action against the workers.[12]

As a result of the signing of the Acuerdo Marco, which was renewed at the start of 1981, and the outcome of the 1980 trade union poll (see below), the CCOO runs the risk of losing its supremacy in the labor world to the UGT. Although the CCOO may be able to block the implementation of the compact in many plants, it will be able to do so only by taking a radical stand on the issues involved and by promoting strikes. This would be damaging to the CCOO, especially because a worsening of the economic situation would warrant a more moderate stand not only in the eyes of the public, management, and government, but also in those of the workers.

The CCOO tried to recover lost ground by signing an agreement with the Employers Confederation of Small and Medium-Sized Firms (Confederación de Pequeñas y Medias Empresas— COPYME).[13] This move failed, however, to bring much advantage to the CCOO because most of the workers in small- and medium-sized firms are not unionized. The CCOO has, in most cases, been unable to breach the 16 percent limit in pay hikes. Notable exceptions have been the 18 percent pay increase for the 10,200 workers at the United States-owned Ford vehicle producers plant and the 18.6 percent pay hike at Maggs, a Nestlé subsidiary.

---

[12] *Ibid.*

[13] "Spain: Focus on New Central Compact," *European Industrial Relations Review*, No. 74 (March 1980), p. 12.

LATEST TRADE UNION ELECTIONS AND OTHER RECENT EVENTS

The bitter fight for dominance in the labor world took a somewhat unexpected turn during the latest trade union elections, held between October 15 and December 31, 1980. The UGT greatly increased its number of elected candidates and thus pulled close to the CCOO, which lost a substantial amount of its past gains.

Tables V-5 and V-6 and Figure V-1 give a clear picture of what the UGT calls its electoral triumph, including a very interesting

TABLE V-5
Results of the 1980 Trade Union Elections and Comparison with the 1978 Elections [a]

Trade Union	1980 Delegates	1980 Percent	1978 Delegates	1978 Percent
CCOO	48,578	30.92	66,006	34.5
UGT	47,502	30.24	41,419	21.6
USO	13,677	8.71	7,203	3.7
Unaffiliated	26,617	16.94	58,329	30.2
Nationalist Groups (ELA/STV, ING, SOC, etc.)	6,427	4.09	1,929 [b]	1.0 [b]
Other Trade Union Confederations	14,298	9.10	18,226	9.44

Source: UGT report on the elections, obtained from the Labor Office of the Spanish Embassy in Washington, D.C.
[a] Discrepancies with Table V-5 are due to different reporting techniques.
[b] Figures for ELA/STV only.

TABLE V-6
Regional Results of the 1980 Elections
(percent of vote and number of delegates elected)

Province	UGT	CCOO	USO	Unaffiliated	Others	Nationalist Unions
Andalucia	38.9%	37.3%	4.3%	10.2%	9.3%	—
	6,662	6,388	730	1,746	1,594	—
Aragon	29.0%	28.8%	12.7%	21.3%	8.1%	—
	1,625	1,614	713	1,191	452	—
Asturias	38.8%	38.6%	4.0%	11.7%	6.0%	—
	2,006	1,994	209	609	315	—
Balearic Islands	34.9%	34.8%	11.8%	11.0%	7.5%	—
	1,202	1,199	406	380	257	—

TABLE V-6 (continued)

Province	UGT	CCOO	USO	Unaffiliated	Others	Nationalist Unions
Canary Islands	35.0%	18.3%	9.8%	10.3%	10.2%	16.4%
	2,200	1,147	617	647	639	1,027
Cantabria	41.2%	26.4%	9.4%	11.6%	11.2%	—
	1,074	687	245	302	293	—
Castile-Leon	35.3%	25.8%	12.7%	15.4%	10.6%	—
	2,882	2,103	1,039	1,253	866	—
Castile-Mancha	35.4%	33.3%	13.4%	9.5%	8.2%	—
	1,651	1,554	628	442	383	—
Catalonia	26.4%	35.2%	10.1%	22.7%	5.6%	—
	8,481	11,299	3,257	7,284	1,781	—
Ceuta and Melilla	54.7%	22.6%	5.6%	15.1%	6.6%	—
	116	48	12	32	14	—
Basque Region (Alava, Guipuzcoa, Vizcaya)	20.3%	17.7%	3.7%	21.0%	12.2%	24.8%
	2,906	2,537	536	3,004	1,744	3,538
Extremadure	37.1%	19.0%	20.1%	11.4%	12.4%	—
	789	403	428	243	263	—
Galicia	24.6%	26.0%	7.2%	14.9%	9.7%	17.3%
	2,384	2,525	707	1,449	945	1,679
Madrid	25.0%	34.3%	4.3%	24.5%	11.9%	—
	4,689	6,435	798	4,592	2,226	—
Murcia	36.9%	29.2%	19.4%	5.3%	9.3%	—
	1,495	1,181	785	213	375	—
Navarre	15.4%	9.2%	12.16%	33.38%	21.7%	8.12%
	347	208	274	752	489	183
Rioja	32.3%	20.8%	16.3%	17.7%	12.6%	—
	415	268	210	228	162	—
Valencian Region	33.9%	36%	10.7%	11.6%	7.7%	—
	6,578	6,988	2,083	2,250	1,500	—

Source: UGT report on the elections, obtained from the Labor Office of the Spanish Embassy in Washington, D.C.

110   Spain

FIGURE V-1
Winners of Trade Union Elections (1980)
(by Province)

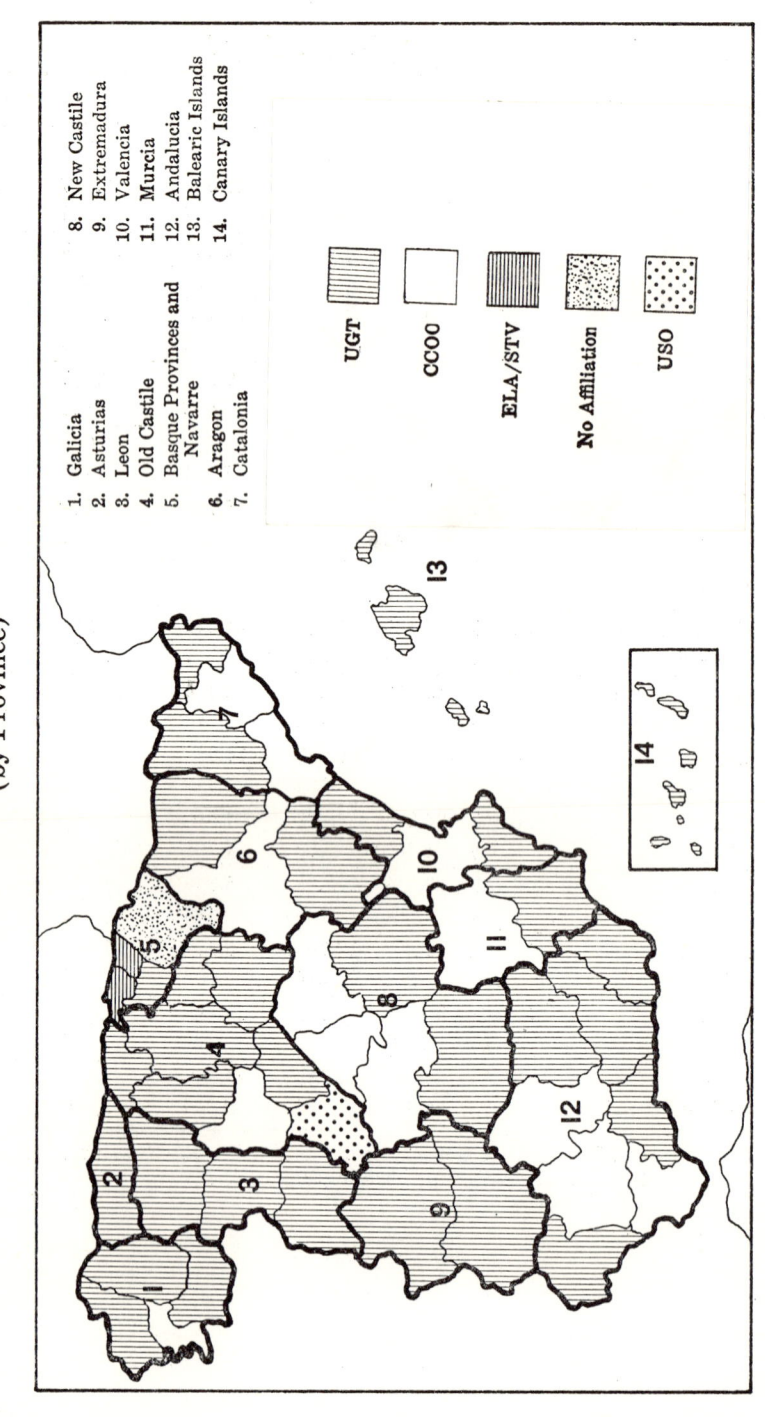

1. Galicia
2. Asturias
3. Leon
4. Old Castile
5. Basque Provinces and Navarre
6. Aragon
7. Catalonia
8. New Castile
9. Extremadura
10. Valencia
11. Murcia
12. Andalucia
13. Balearic Islands
14. Canary Islands

UGT
CCOO
ELA/STV
No Affiliation
USO

Organized Labor in Spain 111

regional breakdown. The UGT has emerged as the political winner of these elections because it managed to break the strategy of the CCOO, which planned to consolidate its hegemony in labor.[14] The UGT won support for its policy of peaceful bargaining with the employers, which had resulted in the signing of the Acuerdo Marco with the CEOE at the start of 1980 and its renewal for 1981.

Another important outcome of these elections has been the failure of the USO to establish itself as the "third syndical force." Although the number of votes received by the USO greatly increased, it was unable to overcome the 10 percent hurdle required by the Workers' Statute to participate in the collective bargaining process. The USO reaped disappointing results even though it had received governmental support and even though the number of nonaffiliated delegates diminished greatly. Apparently, the USO was unable to gather most of the undecided votes, which may have gone to the UGT instead.

The UGT has continued its politics of "responsible acción, of action looking for results, without demagogy, adapted perfectly to the context of economic crisis and to the high unemployment problem," [15] by renewing the Acuerdo Marco for 1981.

The CEOE-UGT pact of 1981 calls for 11-15 percent salary increases based on a 14 percent inflation rate. The compact contains clauses that would allow for an upward revision of the salary hikes should the inflation rate exceed 14 percent. The 11-15 percent increases would be slightly lower than the 15 percent average wage increases of 1980.[16]

In addition, and this is perhaps one of the more important achievements of the two Acuerdo Marcos, there are provisions in these compacts dealing with productivity and absenteeism. The government states that (1) methods for determining acceptable productivity levels should be agreed upon jointly by the two bargaining partners; (2) income generated from productivity increases should be "used to restore company profitability and fund new investments as a means of creating more jobs; and (3) provisions aimed at reducing absenteeism should be included in collective agreements at all levels." [17]

---

[14] Author's translation, "Elecciones Sindicales 80," text of a UGT memorandum obtained by author from the Spanish Labor Office, Washington, D.C.

[15] *Ibid.*

[16] *Liaisons Sociales: Bref Social*, No. 8431, February 4, 1981.

[17] "Spain: Negotiating on Productivity and Absenteeism," *European Industrial Relations Review*, No. 88 (May 1981), p. 6.

The CCOO again refused to take part in the negotiations and in the signing of the compact. But the CEOE-UGT wage pact is still expected to set the norm for collective bargaining in 1981, as it did in 1980, in combination with the new tripartite agreement signed in June 1981 (see below) between the CEOE, the government, and both the UGT and the CCOO.

As far as the public sector is concerned, the government has set a benchmark increase of 12 percent for its workers, with a further 0.5 percent increase permitted to cover productivity deals for 1981. The government maintains that earnings should absorb that portion of inflation caused by higher energy costs.[18]

It is easy to imagine that such proposals will meet with much resistance from the union front. As already mentioned, however, the stands of both the UGT and the CCOO are softening up considerably. This is partly due to the negative results obtained in the latest trade union polls by the CCOO, which traditionally has adopted a more militant approach than its socialist rival. Recently, Marcelino Camacho Abad resigned as deputy of the PCE to concentrate on his trade union job. As head of the CCOO he will try to develop a new strategy to recoup recent losses. In addition, he will try to avoid a threatened split within the CCOO. That split may occur because some union leaders want to pursue a militant policy despite the recession and the setback at the polls, while others would like to see a more direct realignment with the UGT.[19] In general, it seems safe to say that the time is past for large wage increases and that both employers and unions will have to show some restraint to concertedly help the Spanish economy.

> The truth of the matter is that the faltering economy has belatedly brought a grudging acceptance of the need for higher productivity, and an improvement in Spain's appalling absenteeism figures. Mr. Camacho may hold the key to a switch of union priorities from wage-rises to jobs. The UGT dare not leave itself open to communist charges of taking a soft line on pay, but both unions appreciate the shadow over this year's coming round of pay negotiations. Unemployment is running at 12% and is certain to worsen. Savage job cuts are on the way in many industries. At two big car makers 31,000 workers are on short time. Some construction firms and manufacturers of textiles and electrical appliances say that they are close to breaking point. INI, the state holding com-

---

[18] Robert Graham, "Annual Spanish talks open," *Financial Times*, January 8, 1981, p. 2.

[19] *Ibid.*

pany, admits that it has 50,000 too many employees. This includes 10,000 too many on the Seat payroll, 6,500 in shipbuilding, 3,000 with Iberia airlines, 5,000 in steel.[20]

June 1981 Tripartite Agreement

Further proof of the above is the latest wage and price agreement concluded in June 1981 between the government, the employers' confederation, and the UGT and the CCOO. Aside from the terms, the most surprising element of this agreement is the participation of the CCOO, which until the June agreement had remained aloof of any discussion between the CEOE and the UGT, even though it had repeatedly been asked to participate in the talks. The participation of the CCOO came just after PCE leader Santiago Carillo successfully withstood a strong assault by a dissident faction within the party that was trying to give the PCE a more pro-Moscow bent than it has so far had.

The terms of this tripartite agreement are as follows:

> Unions and employers have agreed to rises next year of 9-11%, with a vague commitment to review these increases after six months, in the light of changes in the cost of living. If 9-11% actually happens, it will continue a decelerating pattern. Hourly earnings rose by 26% (1978), 24% (1979) and 19% (1980).
>
> In return, the unions won most of what they asked for on jobs. The government says it will prevent any further rise in unemployment between now and the end of 1982, which in effect means creating 350,000 new jobs. It has promised to pay special attention to the plight of rural workers, pump an extra $220m into the community employment fund this year, allocate $160m for the most needy people, provide extra health service cover and extend the period for dole payments. Efforts will be made to reduce overtime, provide places for school-leavers, encourage early retirement, and stop public servants from holding two or more jobs, a common and lucrative practice.[21]

In addition, the pact will encourage through lower-level collective bargaining negotiations the widespread adoption of "checkoff" rules for the automatic deduction of union dues by the employers. In January 1982 the minimum wage will be revised under the agreement; it now stands at 832 pesetas per day. Finally, a special fund will be set up to help the unemployed suffering from "personal hardship." The fund will amount to 15,000 million

---

[20] "Fraternal Discord," *The Economist*, January 31, 1981, p. 61.

[21] "Spanish Wages: We Promise to be Very Good," *The Economist*, June 13, 1981, pp. 70-71.

pesetas and will be financed forty/sixty by the state and employers, respectively.[22]

"As a footnote, it may be noted that on the day the new Pact was signed, the Government announced that 2400 million pesetas would be paid to the union movement over the next three years by way of compensation for the confiscation of union assets during the Franco era."[23] This would seem to be a setback for the UGT, which believes it should be the sole beneficiary of any compensation from the government, as already discussed above in relation to the conflict over the Casas del Pueblo between the UGT and the CCOO.

Many of the promises made by the government will, however, be very hard to keep. It therefore seems as if the unions have agreed to a decrease in real wages without getting a clear gain in return, except a firm commitment from Premier Calvo Sotelo to prevent a further rise in unemployment.

With a squeeze in real wages and a depressed economy in Western Europe (to which 60 percent of Spanish exports are directed), it will be very difficult for Spain's economic situation to improve in the near future, notwithstanding the devaluation of the peseta, which of course will tend to make Spanish goods more competitive abroad. The period of real wage gains for Spanish workers may be over, and the definite possibility of a sharp decline in real earning is becoming almost a certainty, as can clearly be seen in Figure V-2.

THE MAJOR LABOR CONFEDERATIONS

This short section intends to familiarize the reader with the ideologies, the aims, the national organization, and the international affiliations of the major Spanish trade union confederations. For a quick synopsis of the leadership, national and international affiliations, and addresses of these confederations, the reader is referred to Tables V-1 to V-3 and Table V-7.

The CCOO

In the communist literature, the CCOO is described as a class trade union, which has a national responsibility to fight against the exploitation of the working class. In its own words, the CCOO should pave the way for tomorrow's socialism with today's organization of the work force. This is the theoretical stand.

---

[22] "Spain: Social Contract Analysis," *European Industrial Relations Review*, No. 91 (August 1981), pp. 5-6.

[23] *Ibid.*

Organized Labor in Spain

FIGURE V-2
Wage, Price, and Productivity Increases In Spain, 1973-1981

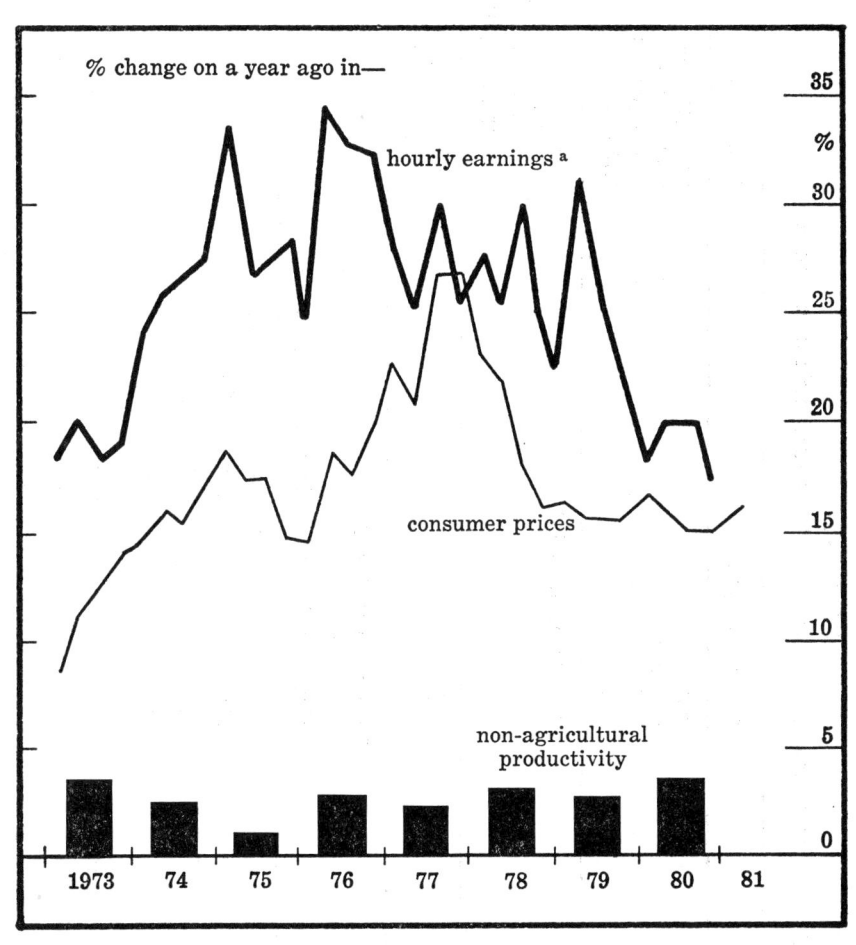

Source: "We Promise to be Very Good," *The Economist,* June 13, 1981, p. 70.
[a] excluding agriculture.

TABLE V-7

The International Trade Unions and Secretariats in Spain

Organization	Affiliates in Spain	Comments
ICFTU	UGT ELA/STV	ELA/STV is the only trade union member of both the WCL and the ICFTU.
WFTU	CCOO (contract only)	One source reports that the CCOO was affiliated with some of the WFTU's TUIs.
ETUC	UGT ELA/STV	The CCOO applied and was refused membership.
EMF	Federación del Metal, ELA/STV Federación Nacional Sidero-metalurgica, UGT	
IMF	Federación Nacional Sidero-Metalurgica, UGT Federación de Trabajadores del Metal, USO	
International Graphical Federation (IGF)	Federación de Artes Graficas, ELA/STV Federación de la Información y Artes Graficas, UGT	
International Secretariat of Entertainment Trade Unions (ISETU)	ELA/STV	

TABLE V-7 (continued)

Organization	Affiliates in Spain	Comments
ITF	Federación de Ferroviarios y Transporte, UGT ELA/STV	
International Federation of Plantation, Agricultural and Allied Workers (IFPAAW)	UGT Federación de Trabajadores Agricolas, ELA/STV	
International Federation of Building and Woodworkers (IFBWW)	Federación de la Construcción y la Madera, UGT Construcción y Madera, ELA/STV	
Miners' International Union	Sindicato Minero, UGT	
Universal Alliance of Diamond Workers	UGT	
International Federation of Air Line Pilots' Association (IFALPA)	Spanish Air Line Pilots' Associations	
ICEF	Federación de la Química, UGT USO Química y Industrias Diversas, ELA/STV	
IUF	Federación del Trabajadores de la Alimentación y Afines, UGT Federación de Trabajadores de la Alimentación y Afines, USO Federación de Trabajadores de la Alimentación y Afines, ELA/STV	

TABLE V-7 (continued)

Organization	Affiliates in Spain	Comments
International Textile, Garment and Leather Workers' Federation (ITGLWF)	Federación del Textil, Confección, Cuero y Calzado, UGT Federación de Trabajadores del Textil Vestuario y Cuero, ELA/STV	
International Federation of Commercial, Clerical, Professional and Technical Employees (FIET)	Federación Nacional de Trabajadores de Banca, UGT ELA/STV	
Public Services International (PSI)	Federación Española de Trabajadores de la Administración Publica, UGT	
Postal, Telegraph, and Telephone International (PTTI)	Federación de Telecommunicaciones, ELA/STV	
International Federation of Free Teachers' Unions (IFFTU)	Federación Española de Trabajadores de la Enseñanza, UGT	
Confédération Internationale des Cadres (CIC)	Confederación General de los Cuadros	Has some contacts with the CIC but no outright affiliation.

Sources: A. P. Coldrick and Philip Jones, *International Directory of the Trade Union Movement* (New York: Facts on File, 1979); *Sindicato Socialista* (Madrid: Edicusa, 1977), p. 76; Cayuelo Miró, Spanish Labor Attaché to the United States, to the author, 1979; direct communication with some of the confederations listed; International Metalworkers' Federation, "Secretariat's Report," *24th World Congress, Munich, October 24-28, 1977*, p. 8; International Graphical Federation, *Twelfth Report of Activities* (Berne: Buch-und Offsetdruck Burkhardt, 1978), p. 59; International Transport Workers' Federation, "Report on Activities 1977-79," *33rd World Congress, Miami, July 17-25, 1980*, p. xiv; International Federation of Plantation, Agricultural and Allied Workers, "List of Affiliates," *4th World Congress, Geneva, December 17-18, 1976*, p. 6; International Federation of Building and Woodworkers, "Documents from the Secretariat," *15th World Congress, Wien, Austria, August 21-24, 1978*, p. 129; International Federation of Airline Pilots' Associations, *Report of the 35th Conference, Brisbane, Australia, April 17-22, 1980*, Appendix G, p. 7; International Federation of Chemical, Energy and General Workers' Unions, "List of Affiliates," *17th Statutory Congress, Mexico City, October 28-31, 1980*; International Union of Food and Allied Workers' Associations, "Executive Committee Meeting, January 23, 1977," *Executive Committee and 18th Congress, Geneva, January 23-28, 1977*; International Federation of Commercial, Clerical, Professional and Technical Employees, "Report on Activities 1973-76," *18th World Congress, Helsinki, August 22-27, 1976*, p. 19; Postal, Telegraph, and Telephone International, "List of Participants," *23rd World Congress, Washington, D.C., October 16-20, 1978*, p. 9; International Federation of Free Teachers' Unions, "Report on Activities 1972-75," *11th World Congress, Florence, December 17-20, 1975*, p. 51.

In practice, the CCOO has adhered to the Moncloa Pact, even though it disagreed with its implementation by the political parties without the direct interpellation of the trade unions. In addition, the CCOO has so far shown a degree of moderation in its leftist stand in keeping with Santiago Carillo's Eurocommunist philosophy.

Recently, the CCOO has asked for higher pay increases than those agreed upon in the UGT-CEOE compact. This is probably more a political than an ideological move. The CCOO is in fact worried that the UGT-CEOE Acuerdo Marco has eroded some of its support and is thus trying to secure its base by getting higher wages for its members than the rival UGT. It may also be largely due to this fear that the CCOO has recently signed the already mentioned government-CEOE-UGT/CCOO pact.

As is true of other "Latin" trade unions (e.g., Italian, Portuguese, and French), a CCOO-affiliated local would find it difficult to survive a prolonged industrial conflict. The membership dues are low, and not more than 50 percent of the CCOO members actually pay them. This is possible because there is not yet a checkoff clause in any of the Spanish bargaining contracts; therefore, no sufficiently large strike fund can be set up, and the CCOO, like other Latin unions, relies on short, paralyzing strikes. Often different sections in one factory will strike on different days, thus paralyzing manufacturing for several days without the strike affecting the whole of the work force. This tactic is often fought by the use of the lockout, which has been declared a legal weapon in the arsenal of Spanish managers, unlike in Italy, for example.

The real pillars of the CCOO's strength are its close political ties with the PCE and the fact that most workers will walk out if a strike is called by the CCOO—whether CCOO members or not—in solidarity.

Nationally the CCOO is organized along industrial and territorial lines. It is divided into Federaciones de Rama, which are more or less what in the United States would be known as industrial unions. In addition, the CCOO is divided into seventeen Confederaciones de Nacionalidad or Uniones Regionales o Provinciales (regional unions). Figure V-3 gives an idea of the internal organization of the CCOO, as well as the organization of the other major federations.

From an international perspective, the CCOO

> reaffirms its desire to be united in the solidarity and the fighting action with all the workers of the world, and to keep special ties

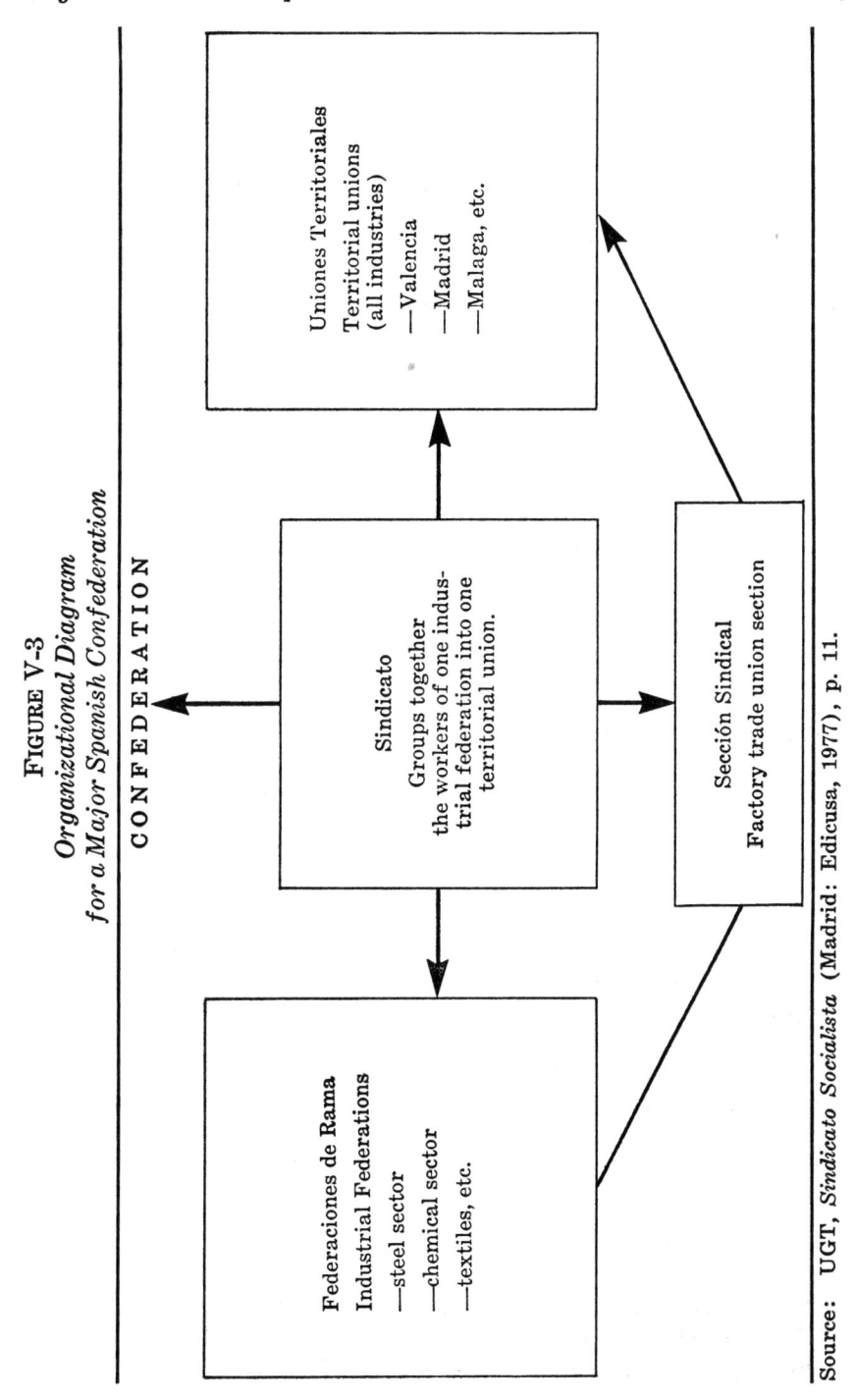

FIGURE V-3
*Organizational Diagram
for a Major Spanish Confederation*

CONFEDERATION

Uniones Territoriales
Territorial unions
(all industries)
—Valencia
—Madrid
—Malaga, etc.

Sindicato
Groups together the workers of one industrial federation into one territorial union.

Federaciones de Rama
Industrial Federations
—steel sector
—chemical sector
—textiles, etc.

Sección Sindical
Factory trade union section

Source: UGT, *Sindicato Socialista* (Madrid: Edicusa, 1977), p. 11.

with the so-called Third World workers and in particular with the workers of Latin America. . . .

Without excluding the international solidarity with workers of the socialist countries and of all the world, we [the CCOO] must give special attention to the unity of the workers of Western Europe.[24]

This statement can be interpreted to mean that the CCOO's main objective in the international field is to join the European Trade Union Confederation (ETUC) and other Western European trade union confederations. The CCOO has, in fact, already applied for membership to the ETUC, into which it stands a good chance of being accepted. This is all the more likely since a precedent has been set by the acceptance of the CCOO's cousin, the Italian Communist General Workers' Confederation (Confederazione Generale Italiana del Lavoro—CGIL).

In regard to the communist World Federation of Trade Unions (WFTU), the CCOO claims in its literature that the WFTU no longer fulfills the needs and aspirations of its workers. For this reason, the CCOO did not join the WFTU, although it did send delegates to observe the WFTU's ninth congress, held in Prague in April 1978.

The UGT

Together with the CNT, the UGT is the oldest Spanish trade union confederation and historical heir of the trade union movement of pre-Franco Spain. Closely linked to the PSOE, it now stands as the second largest trade union in Spain. The UGT made substantial gains in the currently held workers' councils elections in accord with its strong hope to catch up with the CCOO. This hope of advancement was based on the success of the Acuerdo Marco.

Although the CCOO refused to sign the Acuerdo Marco, the USO recently signed the compact, along with the COPYME. "The standing of the compact has recently been given a further boost with a statement from the Chairman of the State holding company, the INI, declaring that public sector firms would apply its provisions, although the INI itself would not sign the compact. (The INI controls around 20% of all Spain's industrial investment.)"[25]

---

[24] Author's translation, *Informe General CCOO, Primer Congreso* (Madrid: Artes Graficas, 1978), pp. 6-8.

[25] "Spain: Focus on New Central Compact," p. 11.

The UGT adhered in practice to the Moncloa Pact, as did the other trade unions, for much the same reasons: a willingness to speed up the "democratization" of Spain coupled with an inability to react negatively due to a structural weakness caused by the too recent return to freedom.

The UGT finds itself in a financial situation similar to that of the CCOO, already described. Its main strength is its affiliation with the PSOE, and of course, its power to call both members and many nonmembers out on strike.

Like the CCOO, the UGT is internally divided into Federaciones de Rama and Uniones Territoriales (see Figure V-3). It was one of the founding members of the International Confederation of Free Trade Unions (ICFTU), is a member of the ETUC and the European Metalworkers' Federation (EMF), and sixteen of its Federaciones de Rama belong to the respective sixteen international trade secretariats (ITSs).

The UGT's political stand is very much akin to that of the PSOE, i.e., of a social democratic mold. This is exemplified by its willingness to compromise with the CEOE in the Acuerdo Marco and by its firm position within the ICFTU.

The USO

Formed from a split with the UGT in 1960, the USO first took part in the CCOO, but then abandoned it because of conflict with the communists in that organization. Some of its members, led by the then secretary general, José Zufiaur, joined the UGT in 1977. Those opposed to unification elected Manuel Zaguirre as the new secretary general and kept the independence of the USO alive.[26]

The USO is the third largest national trade union confederation, shares the financial problems of its two larger rivals, and claims independence from any political influence. Because of opposition from the UGT, it has been unable to affiliate with most of the international trade secretariats, although it did manage to acquire membership in the International Metalworkers' Federation (IMF), the International Union of Food and Allied Workers' Associations (IUF), and the International Federation of Chemical, Energy and General Workers' Unions (ICEF).

The USO claims that it is aconfessional (i.e., it lacks ties with any political organization), and therefore that it does not seek

---

[26] Desotre, *Les Organisations Syndicales*, p. 9.

membership in any of the international trade union confederations (i.e., the ICFTU, WFTU, or the World Confederation of Labor [WCL]). It received some governmental support during the 1980 trade union elections, but still failed to gain more than 10 percent of the votes, the minimum required to take part in the collective bargaining process.

The ELA/STV

The largest and most important of the Spanish regional trade unions, the ELA/STV, is of socialist ideology and sometimes leans very far to the left because of the problems that have disturbed the Basque country recently. A member of both the ICFTU and the WCL and of several international trade secretariats, it claims to fight solely for the welfare of the Basque workers.

CONCLUDING COMMENTS

The Spanish labor movement has come of age since the death of Franco in 1974. Displaying an amazing vitality despite the many years of suppression, Spanish trade unions are now a force to be reckoned with. Whether communist, socialist, or extremist, the various trade union confederations are at a level of organization and strength that favorably compares with their Italian and French counterparts.

At first disorganized and splintered, it now appears that the collective bargaining process in Spain is being nationally organized. Since the formation of the UGT-CEOE compact, there seems to be a tendency toward a simplification of bargaining levels in Spain "with a move away from the present predominance of regional/industry agreements to single national agreements per industry." [27]

This step, together with the realization that more cooperation is needed to bring the country out of the present economic crisis, will hopefully decrease the level of conflict now existing in Spain and avoid great confrontations similar to those that took place in Italy and France in the late sixties.

---

[27] "Spain: Focus on New Central Compact," p. 12.

CHAPTER VI

Conclusion

It is always difficult to conclude an essay that is meant only to convey current conditions in a country. The task seems especially problematic in the case of Spain. There is a definite starting point from which current events can be discussed: the death of Generalissimo Francisco Franco. There is no hint, however, of a point from which one may cast a backward glance. A few months before the resignation of Premier Adolfo Suarez, it seemed that there might have been such a point. Democracy appeared well consolidated, and even the Basque situation could have been viewed with some optimism. Life in Spain seemed to have adjusted to a new rhythm, one closer to that of other Western European states.

Recent events have, however, changed the whole picture. The resignation of Adolfo Suarez was followed by escalating terrorism, a right-wing coup (which fortunately failed), and even more recently, another upsurge of leftist bombings and killings.

The reappearance of the Revolutionary Group of the First of October (Grupo Revolucionario Antifascista Primero Octubre— GRAPO),[1] members of which allegedly killed a general and three Guardia Civil members in two separate attacks on May 4, 1981, added to the tension immensely. The Basque revolutionary group ETA also seems intent on stepping up its terrorist attacks, in an attempt to further destabilize the present democratic government and force the exasperated military to take forceful action. Some members of the latter already tried to subvert the present system during the failed February 1981 coup, and many fear that the next attempt may be successful. Especially disturbing are the claims, often substantiated by indirect evidence, that the ETA is really supported by Moscow, and that it has close ties with the

---

[1] GRAPO is a strange leftist entity; its name refers to the last public appearance of Generalissimo Franco on October 1, 1975.

Irish Republican Army (IRA) and other international terrorist groups.[2]

There are some who claim that this "policy of terror" may already be succeeding in part, and that the army is on the verge of another heavy-handed reaction.

> The regime is now the army's hostage, ... There is a general feeling that although Colonel Tejero and the three or four generals behind him failed to destroy parliament, they put it on a leash. Ministers and politicians must now weigh their speeches and journalists their articles, against possible military reactions.[3]

A military takeover would endanger Spain's entry into both the European Economic Community (EEC) and the North Atlantic Treaty Organization (NATO). Not all prospects are gloomy, however. The king has revealed himself as extremely competent both in times of calm and in times of danger, and Calvo Sotelo, the new prime minister, has managed to restore "a sense of calm and confidence."[4] Perhaps this, coupled with the government's move to the right and the stringent antiterrorist laws that were overwhelmingly passed by the Cortes, may prove to be enough to slowly reestablish peace and tranquillity in Spain.

Although these disturbing events give the impression of a country on the brink of disaster, foreign investors have so far not been frightened away, and the government is implementing a reorganization plan to revamp the textiles, energy, tourist, steel, and automobile sectors. Recently Spain eased its rules on foreign investment; it is hoped that this will spur growth.[5] In addition, discussions are being held between the government and textile manufacturers for a two-billion dollar injection into the textile industry. Productivity is to be increased, and several firms will be absorbed by the state.[6] The large state holdings company, INI, is being reviewed so that "a framework for closer coordination

---

[2] "Victory through the Back Door?" *The Economist*, April 18, 1981, p. 8.

[3] James M. Markam, "Spain's terror: Onus to Soviet," *New York Times*, May 11, 1981, p. A7.

[4] Francisco Basterra, "Repairing the damage to Spain's democracy," *Wall Street Journal*, March 18, 1981, p. 29.

[5] "Spain eases its rules for foreign investment," *Wall Street Journal*, April 14, 1981, p. 34.

[6] Robert Graham, "Pinning hopes on a $2 bn catalyst," *Financial Times*, January 7, 1981, p. 2.

Conclusion

and integration between companies that the state either fully owns or controls"[7] can be achieved.

Many would still argue that Spain is presently in deep trouble, both politically and economically, and that the hopeful signs after the death of Franco have been dispelled by a persistent economic crisis and by waves of both unrest and terrorism. It can also be argued, however, and more rightly so, that things are not as catastrophic as they seem and that they will improve in the near future.

The Spanish people have shown themselves to be very moderate and remarkably constant in their political choices. The governments of both Adolfo Suarez and Calvo Sotelo have successfully steered the country through continuous and pernicious political and economic storms. The king—and this cannot be overemphasized—has kept his cool through several crises and has earned the respect of all those who favor Spanish democracy. Even the workers have shown an amazing sense of balance by heavily giving their support to the moderate, socialist UGT and to its judicious agreements with the Spanish employers' federation. And the labor unions in general have avoided excessive militancy in periods during which militancy might have destabilized the political arena: most notably at the time of the Moncloa Pact—a time of transition—and immediately after the recently attempted military coup.

All these factors must not be underestimated and seem to indicate that Spain may be able to overcome both its political and economic woes in the not-too-distant future. Working toward entry into both NATO and the EEC should provide a stimulus to modernize Spain and keep its democratic makeup intact. And once entry is achieved, actual membership in these two organizations should be a stabilizing factor in itself.

In short, it seems possible to predict a bright future for Spain, a country that has already left its mark on Western civilization and that yet has much to contribute.

---

[7] Robert Graham, "Spain to revamp holdings," *Financial Times*, September 25, 1980, p. 3.

Index

Acuerdo Marco, 106-07, 111-12
Adenauer, Konrad, 26
agriculture sector, 33-36
  EEC standards, 35-36
Alava. *See* Basque provinces
Alfonso XIII, 1, 8
  abdication of, 6
Alianza de la Democracia Socialista, 92
Alianza Popular (AP), 9, 17, 24. *See also* political parties
"alternative on the left," 24
Andalusia, 5, 20
  communist-anarchistic regime in, 93
Andalusian Socialist Party. *See* Partido Socialista Andaluz
Antirevolutionary Group of the First of October. *See* Grupo Revolucionario Antifascista Primero Octubre
AP. *See* Alianza Popular
Arabs
  in Spain, 5
Arafat, Yasir, 22
Aragon, 5
  PAR, 19
Aragonese Regionalist Party. *See* Partido Aragonez Regionalista
Arias Navarro, Carlos, 8, 9, 12
autonomous regions, 16-20, 24
autonomy statutes
  of Andalusia, 20
  of Basque provinces, 20
  of Catalonia, 20
  of Galicia, 20

balance of payments, 46
Bank of Spain, 40
Banking Corporation. *See* Corporación Bancaria
Basque provinces, 1, 5, 11, 13, 18-20. *See also* ETA; ETA/SLV; autonomous regions; autonomy statutes
Blas-Piñar, 17
Bloque Nacional Popular Galego (BNPG), 19. *See also* political parties

BNPG. *See* Bloque Nacional Popular Galego
Bugialli, Paolo, 22, 23

Calvo Sotelo, José, 12
Calvo Sotelo, Leopoldo, 11, 12, 13, 25, 27, 126, 127
  economic policies of, 41, 67, 69
Camacho Abad, Marcelino, 67
  resignation from PCE, 112
Carillo, Santiago, 16, 17, 24
Casas del Pueblo, 93, 114
Castile, 5
Catalonia, 5, 18-20
  communist-anarchistic regime in, 93
  Generalitat, 19
Catalonian Workers' Solidarity. *See* Solidaridad d'Obrera de Catalunya
CCOO. *See* Comisiones Obreras
CD. *See* Coalición Democrática, 17
CEOE. *See* Confederación Española de Organizaciones Empresariales
Ceuta, 22
CFT. *See* Common Foreign Tariff
Charles V, 5
CiU. *See* Convergencia i Unio
Civil War, 6, 7, 8, 11, 13, 22, 93
  and labor legislation, 80
  politics before, 5
  and trade unions, 91, 94
CNT. *See* Confederación Nacional de Trabajo
Coalición Democrática (CD), 17, 25. *See also* political parties
collective bargaining, 84-87
COMECON. *See* Council for Mutual Economic Assistance
Comisiones Obreras (CCOO), 16, 25
  Acuerdo Marco, 106-07, 111-12
  and Casas del Pueblo, 93
  description of, 114, 120, 122
  1978 elections, 102-03
  1980 elections, 108, 111
  formation of, 95
  international ties, 120, 122
  and OSE, 95

and PCE, 120
and PEG, 67
tripartite agreement, 41-42, 113-14
UGT, struggle with, 104-05
Common Foreign Tariff (CFT), 51
communications, 30
communist movement
and CNT, 94
Communist Revolutionary League.
  See Lega Comunista Revolucionaria
Confederación de Pequeñas y Medias
  Empresas (COPYME), 107
Acuerdo Marco, 122
Confederación Española de Derechas
  Autonomas (CEDA), 6. See
  also political parties
Confederación Española de Organizaciones Empresariales
  (CEOE)
pact with UGT, 41, 103, 106-07, 111-12
Confederación Nacional de Trabajo
  (CNT), 92-93
founding of, 92
and UGT, 93
and French CGT, 92
and OSE, 95
Confederación Unitarios de Trabajadores (CSUT), 96
Confederation of the Autonomous
  Right. See Confederación
  Española de Derechas Autonomas
Confederation of Unitary Unions of
  Workers. See Confederación
  Unitarios de Trabajadores
constitution, 80-81
Convergencia i Unio (CiU), 18, 19,
  25. See also political parties
COPYME. See Confederación de
  Pequeñas y Medias Empresas
Corporación Bancaria, 40
Cortes, 9, 13, 18, 19, 22, 24, 126
of Franco era, 94
Council for Mutual Economic Assistance (COMECON), 51
Council of Ministers, 44
court system, labor, 88-89
CSUT. See Confederación Unitarios
  de Trabajadores

Delegación Nacional de Sindicatos
  (DNS), 94
Democratic Coalition, 21, 24
DNS. See Delegación Nacional de
  Sindicatos

Don Juan, 8
d'Estaing, Giscard, 26
economic policies, 41-54
  monetary policies, 42-45
economy
  government participation in, 64-65, 67-69
EE. See Euzkadiko Ezquerra
EEC. See European Economic Community
EFTA. See European Free Trade Association
ELA/STV. See Euska Langilla Alkartasuna-Solidaridad de Trabajadores Vascos
1979 elections, 23
EMF. See European Metalworkers' Federation
Employers' Confederation. See Confederación Española de Organizaciones Empresariales
Employers Confederation of Small and Medium-Sized Firms. See Confederación de Pequeñas y Medias Empresas
energy and fuel resources, 30-32
  nuclear power, 31
  National Energy Plan, 32
ETA. See Euskadi Ta Alkartasuna
ETUC. See European Trade Union Confederation
European Economic Community
  (EEC), 1, 20, 21, 24, 126, 127. See also political parties
entry of Spain into, 21, 72-73
spanish agriculture, 35-36
trade with Spain, 51
European Free Trade Association
  (EFTA), 51
European Metalworkers' Federation
  (EMF), 123
European Trade Union Confederation
  (ETUC)
and CCOO, 122
and UGT, 123
Euska Langilla Alkartasuna-Solidaridad de Trabajadores Vascos (ELA/STV), 93-94
and OSE, 95
description of, 124
Euskadi. See Basque provinces
Euskadi Ta Alkartasuna (ETA), 11, 13, 18, 24, 125. See also political parties
ETA-Militar, 19
and IRA, 26

Index

Euzkadiko Ezquerra (EE), 18. See also political parties

FAI. See Federación Anarquista Iberica
Falange, 8
Federación Anarquista Iberica (FAI), 92
Feranando, 5
foreign relations, 20-22
Franco y Bahamonde, Francisco, 1, 2, 7, 8, 9, 10, 12, 20, 125
  establishes dictatorship, 6

"Galaxia" plot, 11
Galicia, 5, 20
  autonomy statute, 20
Galician National Group. See Bloque Nacional Popular Galego
Galvan, Tierno, 23
Garailkoetxa, Carlos, 18
General Motors, 37
General Workers' Union. See Unión General de Trabajadores
Gonzalez, Felipe, 16, 23, 103
GRAPO. See Grupo Revolucionario Antifascista Primero Octubre
Grupo Revolucionario Antifascista Primero Octubre (GRAPO), 11, 125. See also political parties
Guipuzcoa. See Basque provinces

HB. See Herri Batasuna
Herri Batasuna (HB), 18. See also political parties
historical overview, 5

Iberian Anarchist Federation. See Federación Anarquista Iberica
ICEF. See International Federation of Chemical, Energy and General Workers' Unions
ICFTU. See International Confederation of Free Trade Unions
IMF. See International Metalworkers' Federation
industrial structure, 72-73
industry and manufacturing, 36-39
inflation, 42, 62
infrastructure, 27-40
INI. See Instituto Nacional de Industria
Instituto Nacional de Industria (INI), 3, 4, 38, 67, 122

International Confederation of Free Trade Unions (ICFTU)
  and UGT, 123
  and USO, 124
International Federation of Chemical, Energy and General Workers' Unions (ICEF), 123
International Metalworkers' Federation (IMF), 123
International Union of Food and Allied Workers' Associations (IUF), 123
International Working Men's Association, 92
investment climate, 69-70
investment policies, 69-70
Iribarne, Fraga, 24
Isabel, 5
IUF. See International Union of Food and Allied Workers' Associations

Juan Carlos, 1, 8, 10, 13, 22, 25, 127
  and democratization, 104

Karamanlis, Constantine, 26

labor force
  structure of, 54-57
labor legislation, 75, 79-80, 87-88. See also constitution; Workers' Statute; court system
Labor Ministry, 89
LAFTA. See Latin American Free Trade Association
Latin American Free Trade Association (LAFTA), 51
LCR. See Lega Comunista Revolucionaria
Lega Comunista Revolucionaria (LCR), 17. See also political parties
Leon, 5

Marcos, Rojas, 19
Maria Christina of Australia, 6
Marxists, 7, 11
Melilla, 22
Milans del Bosch, General, 13
Ministry of Commerce
  Higher Price Council, 44
Moncloa Pact, 2, 5, 41, 91, 104, 123, 127
Monzon, Telesforo, 18

National Confederation of Labor. See Confederación Nacional de Trabajo

National Energy Plan (NEP), 32
National Institute of Industry. *See* Instituto Nacional de Industria
National Movement. *See* Falange
National Network of Spanish Railroads. *See* Red Nacional de los Ferrocarriles Españoles
National Trade Union Delegation. *See* Delegación Nacional de Sindicatos
National Union. *See* Unión Nacional
National Workers' Congress, 92
NATO. *See* North Atlantic Treaty Organization
Navarre. *See* Basque provinces
NEP. *See* National Energy Plan
North Atlantic Treaty Organization (NATO), 20, 21, 126, 127. *See also* political parties
entry of Spain into, 2

OPEC. *See* Organization of Petroleum Exporting Countries
Organización Sindical Española (OSE), 94
and trade unions, 95
Organization of Petroleum Exporting Countries (OPEC), 32, 40
Organo Revolucionario de los Trabajadores (ORT), 17. *See also* political parties
ORT. *See* Organo Revolucionario de los Trabajadores
OSE. *See* Organización Sindical Española

Palestine Liberation Organization (PLO), 22. *See also* political parties
PAR. *See* Partido Aragonez Regionalista, 19
Partido Aragonez Regionalista (PAR), 19. *See also* political parties
Partido Comunista Española (PCE), 7, 16, 17, 20, 21, 25
elections procedure, debate over, 104-05
and PEG, 67
and Suarez, 102-03
Workers' Statute, debate over, 104-05
Partido de Trabajadores Española (PTE), 17. *See also* political parties

Partido Nacionalista Vasco (PNV), 18, 25. *See also* political parties
and ELA/STV, 94
Partido Socialista Andaluz (PSA), 18, 19, 25. *See also* political parties
Partido Socialista Obrero Español (PSOE), 7, 9, 11, 16, 17, 20, 21, 25
Partido Socialista Popular (PSP), 23. *See also* political parties
Partido Socialista Unificado de Cataluña (PSUC), 17. *See also* political parties
Party of Spanish Workers. *See* Partido de Trabajadores Español
PCE. *See* Partido Comunista Español
PEG. *See* Programa Económico del Gobierno
Phillip II, 5
PLO. *See* Palestine Liberation Organization
PNV. *See* Partido Nacionalista Vasco
political organization, profile of, 13-15
political parties, 16-20
Popular Socialist Party. *See* Partido Socialista Popular
Popular Alliance. *See* Alianza Popular
Popular Front, 6, 16
Popular Unity. *See* Herri Batasuna
price controls, 42-44
Programa Económico del Gobierno (PEG), 41, 67
PSA. *See* Partido Socialista Andaluz
PSOE. *See* Partido Socialista Obrero Español
PSP. *See* Partido Socialista Popular
PSUC. *See* Partido Socialista Unificado de Cataluña
PTE. *See* Partido de Trabajadores Español
Pujol, Jordi, 18

Red Nacional de los Ferrocarriles Españoles (RENFE), 28
RENFE. *See* Red Nacional de los Ferrocarriles Españoles
Revolutionary Organization of the Workers. *See* Organo Revolucionario de los Trabajadores

Schmidt, Helmut, 26

Index

SEAT. *See* Sociedad Española de Automóviles de Turismo
Second Republic, 6
service sector
  banking sector, 40
  tourism, 39
"sindicatos amarillos," 96
Sindicatos Unitarios (SU), 96
SOC. *See* Solidaridad d'Obrera de Catalunya
Socialist Democratic Alliance. *See* Alianza de la Democracia Socialista
Socialist Workers' Party. *See* Partido Socialista Obrero Español
Sociedad Española de Automóviles de Turismo (SEAT), 38, 86
Solidaridad d'Obrera de Catalunya (SOC), 96
Solidarity of Basque Workers. *See* Euska Langilla Alkartasuna-Solidaridad de Trabajadores Vascos
South American Andean Group, 22
Soviet Union, 22
Spanish-American War of 1898, 6
Spanish Communist Party. *See* Partido Comunista Español
Spanish Parliament. *See* Cortes
Spanish Syndical Organization. *See* Organización Sindical Española
SU. *See* Sindicatos Unitarios
Suarez, Adolfo, 1, 9, 10, 12, 19, 22, 23, 26
  and democratization, 104
  economic policies of, 41, 42-43
  and media, 30
  and PCE, 102-03
  resignation of, 40
  and USO, 95
Syndical Workers' Union. *See* Unión Sindical Obrera

technological development, 38-39
terrorism, 125-26
trade, 51
trade unions
  1978 elections, 102-03
  1980 elections, 198, 111
  history of, 92-95
transportation and port facilities, 28-30

UCD. *See* Unión de Centro Democrático

UN. *See* Unión Nacional
unemployment, 54-55
Union and Convergence. *See* Convergencia i Unio
Unión de Centro Democrático (UCD), 9, 12, 16, 23, 25, 27. *See also* political parties
  and media, 30
  political maneuvering of, 103
Unión del Pueblo Canario (UPC), 19. *See also* political parties
UGT. *See* Unión General del Trabajadores
Unión General de Trabajadores (UGT), 7, 16, 25, 127. *See also* political parties
  Acuerdo Marco, 106-07, 111-12
  and Casas del Pueblo, 93-94
  CCOO, struggle with, 104-05
  and CNT, 92-93
  description of, 122-23
  1978 elections, 102-03
  1980 elections, 108, 111
  founding of, 92
  international ties, 123
  and OSE, 95
  pact with CEOE, 4, 103
  and PEG, 67
  and PSOE, 123
  tripartite agreement, 41, 113-14
  and USO, 103-04
  wage agreements, 41, 42
  and Workers' Statute, 103, 105-06
Union of the Democratic Center (UCD). *See* Unión de Centro Democrático
Unión Nacional (UN), 17. *See also* political parties
Unión Sindical Obrera (USO)
  description of, 123-24
  1980 elections, 111
  formation of, 95
  international ties, 123-24
  and UCD, 95
  and UGT, 95, 103-04
Unitary Unions. *See* Sindicatos Unitarios
United People of Canaria. *See* Unión del Pueblo Canario
United Socialist Party of Catalonia. *See* Partido Socialista Unificado de Cataluña
UPC. *See* Unión del Pueblo Canario
USO. *See* Unión Sindical Obrera

Vizcaya. *See* Basque provinces

wages, 61-62
WCL. *See* World Confederation of Labour
WFTU. *See* World Federation of Trade Unions
Workers' Commissions. *See* Comisiones Obreras
Workers' Statute, 11, 25, 41, 81-82, 103-106
    collective bargaining under, 84-87
    Cortes debate over, 103, 105-06
    and trade unions, 91
World Confederation of Labour (WCL), 124
World Federation of Trade Unions (WFTU), 124
    and CCOO, 122
Zufiaur, José M., 103-04

Racial Policies of American Industry Series

1. *The Negro in the Automobile Industry*, by Herbert R. Northrup. 1968
2. *The Negro in the Aerospace Industry*, by Herbert R. Northrup. 1968
3. *The Negro in the Steel Industry*, by Richard L. Rowan. 1968
4. *The Negro in the Hotel Industry*, by Edward C. Koziara and Karen S. Koziara. 1968
5. *The Negro in the Petroleum Industry*, by Carl B. King and Howard W. Risher, Jr. 1969
6. *The Negro in the Rubber Tire Industry*, by Herbert R. Northrup and Alan B. Batchelder. 1969
7. *The Negro in the Chemical Industry*, by William Howard Quay, Jr. 1969
8. *The Negro in the Paper Industry*, by Herbert R. Northrup. 1969
9. *The Negro in the Banking Industry*, by Armand J. Thieblot, Jr. 1970
10. *The Negro in the Public Utility Industries*, by Bernard E. Anderson. 1970
11. *The Negro in the Insurance Industry*, by Linda P. Fletcher. 1970
12. *The Negro in the Meat Industry*, by Walter A. Fogel. 1970
13. *The Negro in the Tobacco Industry*, by Herbert R. Northrup. 1970
14. *The Negro in the Bituminous Coal Mining Industry*, by Darold T. Barnum. 1970
15. *The Negro in the Trucking Industry*, by Richard D. Leone. 1970
16. *The Negro in the Railroad Industry*, by Howard W. Risher, Jr. 1971
17. *The Negro in the Shipbuilding Industry*, by Lester Rubin. 1970
18. *The Negro in the Urban Transit Industry*, by Philip W. Jeffress. 1970
19. *The Negro in the Lumber Industry*, by John C. Howard. 1970
20. *The Negro in the Textile Industry*, by Richard L. Rowan. 1970
21. *The Negro in the Drug Manufacturing Industry*, by F. Marion Fletcher. 1970
22. *The Negro in the Department Store Industry*, by Charles R. Perry. 1971
23. *The Negro in the Air Transport Industry*, by Herbert R. Northrup et al. 1971
24. *The Negro in the Drugstore Industry*, by F. Marion Fletcher. 1971
25. *The Negro in the Supermarket Industry*, by Gordon F. Bloom and F. Marion Fletcher. 1972
26. *The Negro in the Farm Equipment and Construction Machinery Industry*, by Robert Ozanne. 1972
27. *The Negro in the Electrical Manufacturing Industry*, by Theodore V. Purcell and Daniel P. Mulvey. 1971
28. *The Negro in the Furniture Industry*, by William E. Fulmer. 1973
29. *The Negro in the Longshore Industry*, by Lester Rubin and William S. Swift. 1974
30. *The Negro in the Offshore Maritime Industry*, by William S. Swift. 1974
31. *The Negro in the Apparel Industry*, by Elaine Gale Wrong. 1974

Order from: Kraus Reprint Co., Route 100, Millwood, New York 10546

STUDIES OF NEGRO EMPLOYMENT

Vol. I. *Negro Employment in Basic Industry: A Study of Racial Policies in Six Industries (Automobile, Aerospace, Steel, Rubber Tires, Petroleum, and Chemicals)*, by Herbert R. Northrup, Richard L. Rowan, et al. 1970. *

Vol. II. *Negro Employment in Finance: A Study of Racial Policies in Banking and Insurance*, by Armand J. Thieblot, Jr., and Linda Pickthorne Fletcher. 1970. *

Vol. III. *Negro Employment in Public Utilities: A Study of Racial Policies in the Electric Power, Gas, and Telephone Industries*, by Bernard E. Anderson. 1970. *

Vol. IV. *Negro Employment in Southern Industry: A Study of Racial Policies in the Paper, Lumber, Tobacco, Coal Mining, and Textile Industries*, by Herbert R. Northrup, Richard L. Rowan, et al. 1971. *

Vol. V. *Negro Employment in Land and Air Transport: A Study of Racial Policies in the Railroad, Airline, Trucking, and Urban Transit Industries*, by Herbert R. Northrup, Howard W. Risher, Jr., Richard D. Leone, and Philip W. Jeffress. 1971. $13.50

Vol. VI. *Negro Employment in Retail Trade: A Study of Racial Policies in the Department Store, Drugstore, and Supermarket Industries*, by Gordon F. Bloom, F. Marion Fletcher, and Charles R. Perry. 1972. *

Vol. VII. *Negro Employment in the Maritime Industries: A Study of Racial Policies in the Shipbuilding, Longshore, and Offshore Maritime Industries*, by Lester Rubin, William S. Swift, and Herbert R. Northrup. 1974. *

Vol. VIII. *Black and Other Minority Participation in the All-Volunteer Navy and Marine Corps*, by Herbert R. Northrup, Steven M. DiAntonio, John A. Brinker, and Dale F. Daniel. 1979. *

Order from the Industrial Research Unit
The Wharton School, University of Pennsylvania
Philadelphia, Pennsylvania 19104

* Order these books from University Microfilms, Inc., Attn: Books Editorial Department, 300 North Zeeb Road, Ann Arbor, Michigan 48106.